A must-read for all business owners and brands in the sports and fitness industry

PUNCH ABOVE YOUR WEIGHT

How using a proven, six-step method can help you enhance online visibility, outsmart your competition and win in a digital world.

ISBN:1721601929

Published in 2018.

Printed in the United Kingdom.

What Others Are Saying

"Clear, speaks my language and very informative. As a small business owner, these simple yet effective and well thought out processes will help me develop my business. As Simon advises, it is important to never stop learning and this book is a great way to continue my personal development."

– Seth Amoafo, founder and owner of PASS Abu Dhabi, and community engagement manager for The Special Olympics World Games - Abu Dhabi.

"Simon's book is literally a one-stop shop on what you need to indeed do to 'punch above your weight' and succeed in this crazy fast paced world. Buy it, read it and execute what you've learnt. Your future self and business will thank you for it."

– Simon Jordan, extreme athlete, design and branding consultant, and founder of 5ThingsClear and One Planet One Place.

Contents

DEDICATION

This book is dedicated to everyone in the sports, fitness and leisure industries that continues to make a difference to the lives of individuals and the communities they serve on a daily basis.

Sport has always been a part of my life. It can help form new friendships, break down barriers and help you feel good, both physically and mentally. It helped me to develop physical and mental skills, learn to be a team member, and most of all, have fun.

I'm thankful to my parents for the time and money (and we weren't a wealthy family) they spent during my youth to enable me play as much sport as I could. The number of hours my father spent kicking or bowling a ball at me don't even bear thinking about.

A special mention must also go to my beautiful wife Kerrie for her constant support, and my daughter Daisy – who inspires me to be the best I can every single day – and without whom I would probably have completed this book two months earlier ☺.

INTRODUCTION

As a fellow business owner, I know what's it like to escape corporate or employee life to follow my passion.

We all have different reasons for doing so, but one thing is certain: the uncertainty of entrepreneurship brings with it an incredible sense of freedom, excitement and accountability.

Having worked with SMEs in many different industries since 2009, one of the reasons I diversified into a specialist niche is my passion for sports and fitness. Together with my business partner, we've competed at county league level in football and cricket, and internationally in Karate and American Football competitions, to name a few.

So we took the plunge and decided to combine our personal and professional obsessions. This means each day we help businesses like yours implement the right strategies at the right time, cut through the noise and enhance your visibility, to attract the type of customers *you want* to work with.

In this book I'll be sharing the exact same strategies I use in my business and with clients every day. Strategies that have been developed and honed over the course of 22 years, helping countless clients in the UK, Europe, Asia and the Middle East.

You'll also learn some of the more recent strategic insights and tactics my mentors have taught me. One has run more than 40 companies successfully – with several generating more than a billion dollars a year. While another is an award-winning business leadership coach, author of four number one best selling business books and was listed in the *UK Top 100 Entrepreneur Mentors*, in 2017.

They know exactly what it takes to build a business the right way, implement the right strategies and get the right assets in place to scale a business and enjoy the process.

Just like you, I have to walk-the-walk every day. I know all about the struggles, about feeling overwhelmed, frustrated and time-poor. I've also worked with plenty of clients I didn't like and at times it felt like my entrepreneurial dream was more of a nightmare. I've often questioned whether it was the right decision in the first place.

But in just 12 months that can all change. By following and implementing the steps in this book, steps that have successfully helped build businesses all around the world, you will see a real difference in *your* business.

But I must warn you, this will require work and application. Yes you will be stretched, yes you need to play full out, and yes you need to be committed. But the rewards are there if you do so.

In Part One, you'll discover how and why the business landscape is changing and how you can use it to your advantage. You'll also learn why this is without question the single greatest time ever to build and operate a business.

You'll find out more about some of the key challenges that exist – many of which you may have already encountered in your own business. You'll also learn how to successfully tackle them to help drive growth.

Part Two walks you through each step of a proven six-step method – ASPIRE – in detail. Following these steps over a 12-month period can make a huge difference to your business.

> *"Don't be afraid of failure. This is the way to succeed."*
> — LeBron James

This process is designed to enhance your online visibility, outsmart your competition and help you succeed in a rapidly evolving digital world. It will also help you attract dream clients, accelerate revenue growth, and position you as an expert in your sector.

And then in Part Three, it's all about kicking on and building on the foundations laid during ASPIRE. It explains how by applying the GROW principle, you can elevate your business to even greater heights, but also contribute more and live more. After all, isn't this one of the reasons you started a business in the first place?

You'll also notice that dotted throughout Part One are 'timeouts.' These are ideas, insights and short activities designed to get you thinking about how the principles and strategies you're learning can be applied to your business.

After all, knowing and *not* doing is the same as not knowing.

And don't worry if they take a little time to complete, make you feel uncomfortable or you're unsure what answers to write down. It's all part of the learning and ideas generation process.

Stay with it and don't feel tempted to skip the timeouts, they're there for a reason. This book isn't designed for passive reading, it's more of a educational workbook.

I am firm believer in proper planning prevents poor performance. Being prepared for situations rather than having to 'wing it' gives you the best possible chance to succeed in this digital revolution.

"You were born to be a player. You were meant to be here. This moment is yours."
– Herb Brooks

PART ONE

CRISIS OR OPPORTUNITY?

In Chinese, it's rumoured the word crisis is composed of two characters – one that translates as danger, and one that can be interpreted as opportunity. The original ancient Greek word crisis (spelled krisis) also translates to opportunity.

You could say crisis and opportunity are different sides of the same coin. It's all about what you focus on. For me, a crisis is an opportunity to rise to the occasion, to expedite change, to inspire others.

As someone caught up in the tide of these transformational times, I'm sure you agree that digital technology has and is continuing to change the way we do business. A look back at history tells us the way businesses were run five years ago is no more. A new era is upon us and yesterday is no more.

The question is: do you view it as a crisis or an opportunity?

"It's not whether you get knocked down; it's whether you get up."
— Vince Lombardi

The Times They Are A Changin'

When I was at university in 1994, there were just 4.8 million websites online and only 0.5 per cent of the global population had access to the internet. Today there are well over one billion websites and 47 per cent have access.

So to be more accurate, not only are times a changin' – they've already changed and are only going to continue doing so. And guess what, there's no turning back.

In a relatively short space of time, the internet has transformed the way we communicate, learn and engage. Digital technology has become an integral part of people's lives, particularly Generation Z (those born after 1996) and those towards the end of Generation Y (born between 1977 – 1995).

Many of these individuals are your prospective customers. They are very particular and expect to have online access in all environments at all times. They demand to be connected 24/7, share their experiences and enjoy others' whenever and wherever they want.

And of course, this step-change in behaviour means that as a business, you must also follow suit.

As humans, we often find it challenging to deal with change. Having spoken to many business owners, I know that most feel uncomfortable, unsure or blissfully unaware of what lies ahead.

This is a situation, however, where ignorance *is not* bliss.

"Make each day your masterpiece."
– John Wooden

But there is a positive to all of this. I believe there's never been a *better* time to have your own business.

As a small business you are leaner, faster and more agile than your larger counterparts. The advantage of getting it right in the digital world is that small can also look bigger.

The right branding and digital assets can position you alongside the big boys so that you appear to be punching above your weight.

This is something that prior to the digital revolution would have been impossible for smaller businesses.

And having a marketing strategy and the right systems plugged into far-reaching media channels is no longer reserved for the bigger, more established players in your market. This type of luxury is now available to small business owners and at a fraction of what it used to cost as little as five years ago.

What's happening currently is merely scratching the surface of possibility, with many technologies – despite being 15 or 20 years old – yet to really hit their stride. Exciting times lie ahead for those willing to embrace the inevitability of the digital revolution.

A New Revolution, Unlike Any Other

We're in the midst of a digital era – something that's been coined the Fourth Industrial Revolution.

"Excellence is the gradual result of always striving to do better."
– Pat Riley

In his book of the same title, Professor Klaus Schwab, Founder and Executive Chairman of the World Economic Forum, writes:

"Consider the unlimited possibilities of having billions of people connected by mobile devices, giving rise to unprecedented processing power, storage capabilities and knowledge access."

"We are witnessing profound shifts across all industries, marked by the emergence of new business models, the disruption of incumbents, and the reshaping of production, consumption, transportation and delivery systems. The changes are historic in terms of their size, speed and scope."

One of the greatest threats facing business owners today is not their competition or the economic climate. It's adapting quickly enough to the disruptive forces of this digital revolution.

In 2016, the UK's SME sector lost out on £122 billion in revenue by neglecting the importance of marketing. And despite 76 per cent of British adults using the internet every single day, an ineffective online presence is one of the top three reasons SMEs and start-ups fail.

Understandably, many business owners are still unsure how to approach this revolution. Already busy, suddenly you need to ensure your website isn't lost in the Google jungle.

You also need to think about the impact of mobile phones as a pocket computer and how it's changing the behaviour of your audience.

"I think my secret is that there's no shortcuts for hard work, determination and having that don't give up attitude."
– Jerry Rice

Then there's the worry of standing out amongst your competitors, enhancing your branding, social media and recording videos. Suddenly you have the chance to be accessible to millions of people, but instead many are worrying about how it all fits together.

By approaching this new era in a methodical and focused way, you can ride the crest of the wave. You can expand your reach, provide valuable engagement with your audience, and convert prospects into clients and brand advocates. You'll learn more about how to do this in parts two and three.

There's no question that the digital revolution is here to stay. And despite causing industries to adapt, evolve or become like the dinosaurs, it's also creating new opportunities.

Who would have imagined a decade ago that people would be making a decent living on YouTube and Instagram? Or that you could use an app to hire an on-demand chauffeur, payable on your credit card (Uber), and book unique accommodation anywhere in the world (Airbnb).

You don't even have to develop your own app. Just by simply listening to and engaging with customers online, companies are seeing their businesses grow.

In fact, a study by the European Commission reveals SMEs that actively engage with consumers experience up to 22 per cent higher sales growth than those that don't.

Just consider the impact that could have on *your* business.

"If you have everything under control, you're not moving fast enough."
– Mario Andretti

It Takes Change To Make Change

Change is constant and an ever-present element of our lives – and so it is with business.

Whether positive or not, you still have the same choices: ride the wave or struggle to remain afloat as you procrastinate or feel confused, indecisive and overwhelmed.

It's also worth remembering that the strongest trees grow in the strongest winds, not in the most fertile soil. So if you've been struggling to get to grips with this whole digital marketing thing, don't beat yourself up.

Often we look at individuals that are successful and forget that it didn't happen instantly for them.

In fact there's a famous saying, "*It takes years to become an overnight success.*" How true it is, yet so many people lose patience and give up.

Anyone who has 'made it' likely went through tough times and failed many times. Yet their passion and self belief remained their guiding light throughout.

Take Steve Jobs, for example. When forced out of Apple in 1985, he could have easily felt victimised or bitter. But he chose to see this as an opportunity.

"Live everyday as if it were your last because someday you're going to be right."
– Muhammad Ali

He got straight back to work, purchasing a small animation company from George Lucas – transforming the 40-person outfit into an award winning operation. Oh, and he renamed it – calling it Pixar – perhaps you've heard of them?

After a string of successful productions, The Walt Disney Company acquired Pixar in 2006 for $7.4 billion, making Jobs Disney's largest shareholder.

Now you might be thinking "Yeh, but that's Steve Jobs," but the fact is it's never the event that changes our future, but how we react to the event. The difference between stumbling blocks and stepping stones is how you use them.

Wherever your business is at in the digital revolution (and everyone is different), it's perfectly natural to feel uncomfortable about what lies ahead in the future.

And while it may not feel like it right now, a little discomfort goes a long way to improving your learning, creativity and performance. It's all part of the process.

As kids, we were forever braving new experiences without an ounce of fear. As we get older, we become more routine-oriented and often choose to stay within our comfort zone.

But the very fact that you're reading this book shows that you're adaptable and adventurous enough to want to enhance your online visibility, outsmart your competition, accelerate revenue growth, and succeed in a digital world.

"However ordinary each of us may seem, we are all in some way special, and can do things that are extraordinary, perhaps until then... even thought impossible."
– Sir Roger Bannister

TAKE A TIMEOUT!

Spend a minimum of five minutes thinking about your own business and where it sits on the digital landscape.

On a scale of 1-10 (10 being most prepared), how prepared is your business for the digital revolution?

What are your competitors doing well that you could emulate?

How easily can users find you on the web? (Try some web searches to see where you show up.)

"If you don't have confidence, you'll always find a way not to win."
– Carl Lewis

Take Advantage of Transformational Times

If there's one overriding principle I'd like you to take from this book, it's this: succeeding in the digital revolution is not about implementing digital marketing. It's about marketing effectively in a digital world. There's a subtle, yet crucial difference.

It wasn't too long ago that as an SME, you were at a distinct disadvantage when it came to marketing and technology. Both required significant investment if you were to make a real impact and get your message out to the world, meaning that only the larger, wealthier corporations could afford it.

But in the digital revolution it's different and the marketing and technology landscape has been turned on its head.

Smaller, more agile and connected businesses are now able to compete on a level playing field to outsmart and outmanoeuvre their bigger, slower rivals.

Today, more and more people – just as you have done – are pursuing their passion and turning it into a business. And thanks to digital technology and social media in particular, you can now create a real impact – locally, nationally and internationally.

And it starts with passion. In his book *Become A Key Person Of Influence*, Daniel Priestley alludes to this very point by saying *"If it feels like hard work you will always get trumped by those who have passion."*

"Push yourself again and again. Don't give an inch until the final buzzer sounds."
– Larry Bird

It's passion that convinces you to leave your day job. It's passion that sells you on starting your own business. It's passion that pushes you when the going gets tough.

But I'm sure you believe you can do more, be more, and achieve more. But why hasn't your passion driven you to achieving the success you want?

Because it's not just about what's in your heart; but what's in your head.

There's absolutely no question that without your passion, energy and determination, you wouldn't be where you are today. But it requires more – particularly in these new, transformational times.

You know you can do the functional aspects of your job – those that occur day in, day out – in your sleep. That's one of the reasons you started your business.

However, on top of the aspects you know and love well, there are other tasks. Admin, accounting, IT, sales and marketing, and more all need to be done to a high level. At times, it can seem like you're spinning plates and you daren't drop any.

Suddenly, you're hustling day in, day out, and it feels like a chore, rather than building your empire. The excitement you had at the start begins to turn in to exhaustion, frustration and in some cases, desperation.

Whilst you don't (and indeed shouldn't) necessarily have to get deeply entrenched in every single detail related to these other tasks – all of which are important in their own right – some top line insight is advisable.

"Age is no barrier. It's a limitation you put on your mind."
– Jackie Joyner-Kersee

But when it comes to their daily management, I highly recommend you farm them out to those with the necessary expertise. You can always earn more money but you can't buy more time.

In fact according to 2016 UK Government statistics, 49 per cent of SMEs suffered from the effects of a digital skills gap. Being a business owner or entrepreneur doesn't mean you have to be a one-person show. Yes it's *your* show and you may well be the face of the business too, but don't get bogged down in the mire and feel you need to be a jack-of-all-trades.

With so much to do, it can get overwhelming. And whilst it's tempting to bootstrap it and do it all yourself, what invariably happens is you are not as productive as you want or should be.

Spread too thinly, you can become frustrated that the core of your business isn't performing to an optimal level.

And those peripheral tasks you're also juggling are never completed in the time or to the quality that you wanted in the first place.

Which is why, whatever business you're in, I'm always preaching that business is a team sport. And I know from bitter experience, too.

More about that later.

"If you can believe it, the mind can achieve it."
– Ronnie Lott

Having a supporting cast – even on a temporary or contract basis – allows you to dedicate time to learning more so that you can create more. This in turn enables you to develop more so that you can produce more, and implement more so that you can deliver more.

It frees up your time to focus on the stuff you *should* do, not the stuff you feel you *need* to do, given there's no one else to do it. And there are so many specialists out there looking for freelance and contract work, you'll be spoiled for choice.

It's also not as expensive as you might think, given that you can pay people by the hour, instead of committing to days or weeks of work in advance.

But if you are on a shoestring to begin with, I have a solution for you in Part Two, where I explain how you can get people to work with you for free.

And it's all perfectly above board and a win/win situation for both parties.

There are many examples in history that illustrate why you must be prepared and adapt to what's coming. You only need to look at the transitions from previous industrial revolutions. From the agricultural age to steam power and factories to automated assembly lines, progress is constant.

It really is evolve or die.

In reality, the digital revolution is more 'here and now' than 'what's coming' – and of course, technology will continue to evolve. But many businesses – even the big boys – haven't yet grasped the immediacy.

> *"All great empires die from within."*
> – Terry Bradshaw

It's here, it's real and it's causing casualties. Think about Woolworths, Comet and Toys R Us to name just three. Trying to swim against the current or letting it sweep you away by surprise are both fast tracks to failure.

Throughout this book, you're going to acquire much of the knowledge you and your team need to help elevate your business, differentiate your brand and attract more of the type of customers you want. Look at this book as the lifeboat to helping you navigate the current of the digital revolution.

Part of your journey through this book and across the digital landscape will involve a great deal of learning. However, I am keeping it as simple as possible for you. Whilst leaving practically no stone unturned, it is designed so you can quickly understand and know how and where you need to take action first.

Lies, Damned Lies And Statistics

In over two decades of working with SMEs, large regional companies and multinational giants, I've heard a number of common misconceptions, including:

"We're too small to use digital marketing." "A great website is all we need." "We need lots of social media followers to succeed so it's not worth it."

"But don't you have to be on every social channel to make it worth it?" "We just don't have the resources." "I'd heard SEO is no longer important." "Our audience isn't online, they're too old." "Everyone knows us, so why bother!?"

"If you can't outplay them, outwork them."
– Ben Hogan

SMEs accounted for a combined annual turnover of £1.8 trillion in 2016 – 47 per cent of all UK private sector turnover.

But less than one per cent of SMEs registered since 2012 have managed to achieve consistent, sustainable growth.

It goes without saying that marketing is essential to finding new audiences, enhancing reach, and exploring opportunities. However, while bigger companies are able to assemble large, dedicated teams, SMEs cannot always afford to.

Instead, you must use your size and agility to your advantage.

The digital landscape is a crowded place with your competitors fighting to be heard. On top of this, the flood of messages we encounter every single day is causing attention spans to diminish.

So it's imperative that you stand out and cut through the noise.

As you'll discover later in this book, it's about focusing and coordinating your marketing efforts – and doing so quickly and decisively.

By having the right knowledge and framework in place, you will find the entire process easier, more productive and results oriented.

You must remember it's a marathon, not a sprint. You should test things to see if they can be improved (clue: invariably they can).

"The key to winning is poise under stress."
– Paul Brown

I also believe you should develop a presence on one or two social media platforms and create engaged communities first, before moving onto more platforms.

And despite what you may have heard or seen with celebrities and their six and seven-figure followings, don't worry too much about numbers of fans and followers.

A buzzing community of 1,500 that connects with your brand is worth more to you than 15,000 that don't.

As the business leader and face of your brand, you might feel the challenges you have are yours and yours alone. But as I've already alluded to, I believe even if you're a sole trader, business is a team sport.

So why not involve someone you know or trust who can provide a fresh pair of eyes and help you produce new ideas and overcome your obstacles?

Whilst change brings with it uncertainty – and a fear of the unknown – we already live in an ever-changing world. A world where on a daily basis we're bombarded with new information, knowledge, experiences, technology and of course, challenges.

In the digital revolution, the new currency is people's attention. You need to be seen, engaged with and proactively working towards improving your visibility every day.

What occurred yesterday has gone. Today is a new day and a new opportunity. But such an opportunity comes with a caveat.

> "It is not the size of a man but the size of his heart that matters."
> – Evander Holyfield

It's essential that you continue to adapt, get out of your comfort zone and be consistent in your actions. As you've already read and I'm sure you already knew, the risk for not doing so is to suffer extinction.

This is not just a success skill, but a survival skill too.

TAKE A TIMEOUT!

Spend 10 to 15 minutes thinking about where your business is currently and where you'd like it to be in the future.

What tasks do you do that stop you from giving more value where it's needed?

Do you currently have part-time or contract staff? Could you use more?

What business functions could you automate by using technology?

Notes:

"You miss 100 percent of the shots you don't take."
– Wayne Gretzky

Does Your Website Work For You?

And I mean *really* work for you? Your website can and should do many things. It can position you as a key person in your industry and differentiate you from your competitors. It can emphasise your credentials and instil your audience with confidence, trust and knowledge.

It can be your online brochure, showcasing your products and services. It should explain who you are and how you solve your target audience's problems, pain points and frustrations.

Whether you're a large corporation or a one-man band, it's an integral and irreplaceable component of an effective marketing strategy. However, in business – as in sports and fitness – it's all about preparation, game plan and execution.

I'm obsessed with ensuring every asset a business has works to its full potential. Your website – particularly in the digital revolution – is no different.

After all, although you may not build it yourself, you invest a not insignificant amount of time and money contributing to its messaging, imagery, and the end result.

And as it's essentially your shop window, available to view 24/7/365, why wouldn't you make it work its socks off for you?

I've worked with dozens of clients who had beautifully aesthetic websites built by designers they know and trust. But as I dug a little deeper, I encountered the same challenge.

"I don't want to be the next Michael Jordan, I only want to be Kobe Bryant."
– Kobe Bryant

Although these clients were happy with the look and feel of their site, they were at a loss as to why they weren't attracting more visitors and generating more business.

The key with any tactical asset such as your website, is to be clear on its purpose before you even have one line of code written.

What do you want it to achieve? Who is it aimed at? Where do you want to take the visitor once they reach your site?

Once you've defined its objectives, you can begin to reverse engineer each objective and reflect this in the design and content of your site. It's a bit like designing a gym.

You wouldn't just buy all the equipment you need and place it just anywhere. You'd plan it out by having cardio machines together and mirrors where the free weights will be located.

You might have a separate studio for spinning, pilates and yoga classes. And a café near to the entrance, where it's highly visible.

It's no different with a website – it should planned accordingly.

Ideally you should be putting the visitor at the centre of your site's content. It should speak their language (familiar tone of voice, type of words they use), address their challenges (demonstrates you understand them) and offer the right solutions.

"It is better to fail aiming high than to succeed aiming low."
– Bill Nicholson

But more often than not, they're built with a primary focus on the business itself. They talk about the business, its owner and how good they both are.

The result: visitor numbers, repeat visitors, engagement, and lead generation suffer.

This often requires a 180-degree shift in a business owner's perspective on marketing and exactly what purpose their website should serve. But once they realise, they often experience a genuine 'eureka' moment.

You can even see it in their body language and facial

expression as realisation hits home and the penny drops.

So, let's assume you've agreed on your new website's objectives and your designer has all the right visual and branding elements in place.

Here are six essentials that in my opinion, your website should have:

1. **Content that's engaging and useful**
   This maximises your chances of being noticed ahead of your competitors and helps you to develop a loyal following. Firstly you need to grab your audience's attention by identifying exactly how you can help them (see point two below).

"You have got to shoot, otherwise you can't score."
– Johan Cruyff

Then you need to develop rapport and encourage them to explore your site further (point five elaborates on how to do this). Finally, ensure your site has a range of insightful content so that you are seen as the go-to resource or expert in your industry.

2. **Clear value proposition**
   How do you solve your audience's problems? Why should they use you instead of one of your competitors? What makes you unique? What benefits do you deliver? This is your chance to differentiate yourself, wear your heart on your sleeve and carve out a niche for yourself in terms of a following. Clue: be *you*.

3. **A means of capturing names and email addresses**
   This might be the single most popular faux pas I see from small businesses. This gives you an opportunity to enhance the relationship further by providing valuable advice, information and expertise. It also allows you to market through email until they're ready to buy and gives you an asset – their email address. But don't abuse this privilege.

4. **Calls to action**
   These help you to guide your website visitors through your site or to take specific actions and should vary for each stage of the buying cycle. So for example you could include phrases such as: *"free consultation," "watch video," "request information," "subscribe to newsletter,"* or *"receive 10 per cent off your first order."*

   "You're never a loser until you quit trying."
   – Mike Ditka

5. **Inform or offer value on every page**
   I am a big believer in the adage *"the more you give, the more you'll receive."* This should be done with authenticity and a genuine desire to help your audience.

   You may have a series of videos you can use on various pages, or special insights you can compile into free downloadable products (more about the power of this later). Also, you should always talk from their point of view and describe exactly how you can help them.

6. **Analytics (behind the scenes)**
   Data is important but is often overlooked as it's considered boring and purely number crunching. But knowledge of where your visitors are coming from and how they're behaving once they reach your site is critical to enhancing your digital strategy. What is measured can be improved – don't guess.

You want your personality to shine through into your website, so content should be genuine, helpful and deliver value. By doing so, you'll not only start to see more visitors, engagement, downloads of your free products and email subscribers – you'll build more and more trust.

Clarity is also important. Having simple navigation and an uncluttered appearance makes life easy for your visitors. When people can't find what they're looking for, they get frustrated. And when they get frustrated, they leave your site.

But you also have to take into a consideration another, very important aspect of the digital landscape.

> *"The man who has no imagination has no wings."*
> – Muhammad Ali

The next time you're in any public space – it may even happen where you're working – look around you. What are people doing? That's right, they're glued to their phones.

Why You Need To Be Mobile

The launch of the first generation iPhone in 2007 changed the rules of engagement for all businesses. The smart phone has placed a PC in people's pockets, ensuring that (with a few exceptions) wherever you are and whenever you want, you can be connected with ease and convenience.

Smart phones and tablets are now the most popular devices people use to access the internet. And whilst it's still early days, the trend appears to be irreversible. The digital world is switching from desk to pocket.

According to Statcounter, less than five per cent of pages were loaded on mobile devices in 2010. By 2013, that figure was just under 25 per cent.

Today, over half of webpages globally are viewed on mobile phones or tablets.

And with enhanced processing power, increased battery life, faster network speeds, and larger screen sizes, the transition from desktop to mobile is continuing to accelerate. This is where every business needs to be focusing. Period.

Each year, another wave of mobile devices is unleashed – more powerful and versatile than the generation before. These days, anyone with a current model smartphone or tablet can pretty much perform every task their desktop PC can handle, but with added convenience.

"The more I practice, the luckier I get."
– Gary Player

There is however, another important consideration you need to be aware of, one that can dramatically affect your business. The behaviour of mobile users is different to their desktop PC counterparts.

They have different objectives to desktop users, often wanting information in quick, easily digestible bites.

Mobile purchases are often more impulsive in nature, and some statistics reveal that mobile users spend more per purchase than those on a desktop.

This is critical insight into the behaviour of consumers – some of which will be your target audience.

And although there are slight variances across age groups, the long-term picture is we're definitely ditching desktop for mobile.

Even my 70-year-old father-in-law uses his mobile more than his MacBook.

So, how can you use this to your advantage and tailor your online presence and visibility accordingly? The answer is by adapting your website and your social media activity.

And studies show that *not* doing so results in you short changing your visitor's experience of your business and leaving a lot of money on the table.

Before we look at social media, let's discuss why making changes to your website can help drive growth to your bottom line.

"I'm a very positive thinker, and I think that is what helps me the most in difficult moments."
– Roger Federer

Is Your Business Mobile Friendly?

Web design has evolved exponentially during the past decade. Back in the 'dark ages' of 2007, they were predominantly built using table layouts, Adobe Flash and masses of gimmicks, bells and whistles.

The good news is, as technology has developed, so have design capabilities and with it, what is known as user experience – UX for short. This means the cluttered, clunky websites of yesteryear have made way for minimalistic, beautiful designs with effortless navigation.

In recent years, as mobile has grown in popularity, web design has adapted, too. And for good reason: desktop-friendly websites do not load the same way on a mobile. Without getting too technical, here are three key reasons why:

1. Difference in screen size

A phone's screen is typically three to six inches diagonally (although some are larger), with tablets varying in size from nine to 12 inches. Desktop PCs on the other hand can be anywhere between 20 and 30 inches, with laptops and notebooks 13 to 17 inches.

Having a smaller screen affects the layout of your site, the navigation and quantity of content you should have. A mobile website will adjust all these elements accordingly. Ignore these facts at your peril!

"I've failed over and over and over again in my life and that is why I succeed."
– Michael Jordan

2. Text can appear small or difficult to read

Mobile websites are specifically designed and scaled so they display text, images and clickable buttons beautifully on a smaller screen. Desktop sites don't have this capability, making it extremely difficult for users to read, watch and understand your content.

3. Navigation and functionality

Clicking a link with a mouse using your desktop or laptop is easy, right? But trying to tap the same link on your mobile's keypad with sausage fingers can be more of a challenge.

So for mobile users, it's a great idea to replace these fiddly text links with touch-friendly buttons that make everyone's life easier. It'll also help those who want to explore your site further and request information.

All in all, you're enhancing your visitor's experience, which is one of the major boxes you want to tick. And although you need to do more than just this to be memorable, not doing it is a sure-fire way to be memorable for the wrong reasons.

By optimising your website for mobile, you can ensure, regardless of the device being used, you're delivering a seamless experience to your web visitors.

But here's another, more important consideration: a site *not* optimised for mobile will also load a lot more slowly on your phone.

"Champions keep playing until they get it right."
– Billie Jean King

Statistics show as many as 57 per cent of mobile users leave a website if it takes more than three seconds to load.

And 30 per cent will abandon a purchase if the shopping cart isn't optimised for mobile devices. As you can see the stakes are high.

The UK has one of the highest mobile penetration rates globally, with 66 per cent of the just over 60 million internet users regularly using their mobile to get online. But if your website isn't mobile-friendly, you'll attract less visitors, discourage those that reach your site and ultimately lose potential sales.

Yes, it's important to have an online presence. Yes, it needs to be visible when people are searching for your type of business. And yes, it should look professional.

But mobile is not just the future, it's the present and it's crucial that you ensure your biggest digital asset is taking advantage of that.

You essentially have two different avenues you can pursue:

A Mobile-Dedicated Website

Option one is to keep your current website as is, and have another one built specifically for mobile, together with a separate URL.

So for example, your current (desktop) website might be: mywebsite.co.uk, with your additional mobile site being: m.mywebsite.co.uk – the extra 'm' at the start meaning mobile.

"Football is football and talent is talent. But the mindset of your team makes all the difference."
– Robert Griffin III

This option works well because it detects the device someone is using quickly, redirecting them to either the desktop or mobile version of the website.

To the untrained eye it's unnoticeable.

Another advantage is you can create custom experiences for both options. This is essential due to the difference in screen sizes and user objectives. Here's why:

Although we live in a time-poor society, desktop users are often happier to spend more time browsing and reading. If we're already sat at a desk, we potentially have more time to research than if we're on the go.

Mobile users on the other hand are often on the look out for more specific information.

By the very nature of what a mobile device can give, users often prefer to digest information quickly and in bite-sized chunks.

The downside of having separate websites is you now have to manage two URLs and both versions of content.

In fact the content side of things is perhaps the most arduous, because important changes on one site will most likely need to be applied to the other, doubling the workload.

Cost-wise, this option tends to be a little cheaper upfront. There will however, be periodic, ongoing investment for applying content and other changes, as in the majority of cases they'll need to be applied to both sites.

"I like criticism. It makes you strong."
– LeBron James

A Responsive Design Website

Responsive design refers to a website that looks great and works perfectly whether the user is viewing it on a desktop, laptop, tablet or smart phone.

A one-size-fits-all solution, it delivers an optimal viewing experience for any device or screen size.

It provides a consistent look and feel, great user experience and text is easily readable, without the need for zooming in or horizontal scrolling.

Navigation is also straightforward and there's more than enough space for users to be able to tap on links and buttons with ease.

It's a fluid and flexible layout that automatically adjusts according to the device being used, eliminating the need to have separate websites for desktop and mobile.

And because responsive design operates on just one URL, you only have one set of content to worry about.

Whilst it's the better option in my opinion, the initial investment to build or switch your site to a responsive design is a little higher.

But once everything is in place, ongoing maintenance and content amendments eat up far less time, money and resources, as you only have to take care of one website.

"You have to believe in yourself when no one else does – that makes you a winner right there."
– Venus Williams

In fact Google themselves recommend using a single, responsive design, particularly from a search engine optimisation (SEO) standpoint.

In other words, how visible your website is for people searching online for the products and services you deliver.

The Future?

Whilst you don't immediately need to concern yourself with the next few paragraphs, it's useful for you to understand what's coming around the corner.

With technological advancements and heightened consumer expectations going hand in hand, we can expect some radical changes in the digital ecosystem in the next five to 10 years. This will also apply to the future of web design.

Many experts believe that eventually websites with the ability to support virtual reality will become more and more common.

By providing a realistic three-dimensional environment, web users will be able to explore your site in new, interactive and interesting ways.

A virtual reality-optimised site would create numerous possibilities for you to tell stories, deliver valuable experiences, and engage with your audience.

It would be taking the digital experience to a new level of interactivity, and with it, opportunities for your business.

"You can't afford to live your life with regrets."
– Shane Warne

If you sell sports equipment, apparel or nutrition, imagine someone being able to browse your e-commerce website as if they were standing in a physical outlet.

But they'd be doing so from the comfort of wherever they were at that particular moment and on their chosen device – whether smart TV, laptop, tablet or phone.

Imagine what it could do for you if you have a tennis, football or rugby academy – or even a gym?

Someone visiting your website could (in the virtual world) walk in, look around, inspect your facilities, equipment and familiarise themselves with you and your brand. All of this without setting foot in your premises.

Whilst this technology isn't officially mainstream yet, it's only a matter of time. Something that we may have only envisaged seeing in Hollywood movies *is* the future of digital technology. It's reality.

But for now, concentrate on optimising for mobile.

*"In football as in watchmaking, talent and elegance mean
nothing without rigour and precision."*
– Lionel Messi

TAKE A TIMEOUT!

Spend 10 to 15 minutes and consider the following:

Does your website communicate your true story and values?

Which pages receive the most views? Why do you think that is?

How many leads does your website generate each month?

Notes:

"I don't chase dreams, I hunt goals."
– Conor McGregor

Set Yourself Up For Social Media Success

It's incredible to think that only 12 years ago, social media was just a blip on the digital landscape.

A time when the now defunct MySpace was the most popular social network in the world and Facebook was still in its infancy.

But fast-forward to today and people living in the most remote parts of the world are using Facebook, Twitter, Instagram and Snapchat. We now live in a hyper-connected society where social media is shaping our lives, relationships, decisions and for some, their sense of self.

In his book, *Jab, Jab, Jab, Right Hook: How To Tell Your Story In A Noisy Social World*, Gary Vaynerchuk writes, "*It took 38 years before 50 million people gained access to radios. It took television 13 years to earn an audience that size. It took Instagram a year and a half.*"

Social media is growing at an alarming rate from a consumer point of view. For some it's bordering on addictive. It's also the fastest growing marketing sector, and the trend is showing no signs of slowing down anytime soon.

At the time of writing, almost 93% of the UK population – 60 million people – is fully connected to the internet at home. Many also carry a smart phone around with them wherever they go. Oh, and of that 60 million I mentioned, 42 million are active social media users.

The simple fact is people enjoy the social aspect of consuming and sharing their media, experiences, likes and dislikes. Just take a look at your Facebook, Twitter or Instagram feed – it's relentless.

> *"Everything is practice."*
> – Pelé

And so at this point in the game, if you don't have a strategic and consistent social media presence, you're leaving opportunity and money on the table.

Plus, did you know social media marketing has a 100 per cent higher lead-to-sale rate than outbound marketing?

Social media gives you the ability to foster conversations and engage with different 'communities' locally, nationally and internationally.

And every interaction is an opportunity to intertwine stories about who you are and what your brand stands for.

Don't Follow The Crowd

But all too often businesses prefer to use social media as a platform to get out their metaphoric megaphone. Social is designed for interaction.

If a Facebook, Twitter or Instagram page is just a series of *"me, me, me"* broadcasts, commercial messages and self-promotional posts, it's unlikely to achieve the desired results.

And whilst I (largely) talk about these three platforms in this book, they aren't the only game in town. Pinterest, Snapchat, LinkedIn are among the others available to you and a bunch of interesting voice-based platforms such as Anchor, Bubbly and Listen are emerging.

But to keep things simple and get a foot hold in social media, I often recommend Facebook, Twitter and Instagram.

"The man who can drive himself further once the effort gets painful, is the man who will win."
– Sir Roger Bannister

Successful storytelling not only builds your reputation and brand equity, it develops goodwill in your audience. It also shows you're human – a real person, and not hiding behind a logo or persona.

And the more people get to know, like and trust you, the more likely they are to share your messages – and eventually, buy from you.

Although the average internet user has five social media accounts, does that mean that you should follow suit? Probably not, especially to begin with.

Master one or two in the beginning – ideally where your target audience spends the most time. This means evaluating and understanding your audience should be a priority.

Plus, there's a danger of stretching yourself too thinly and suffering overwhelm – and understandably so.

It's better to have one or two consistently active social accounts, rather than five sporadic ones that only post once in a while.

You should also ensure you optimise your content for each platform.

You wouldn't use a billboard advert on Google Adwords, so why would you duplicate (or automatically cross-post, which is worse) across Facebook, Twitter and Instagram?

Imagine you post on Facebook and use the automatic cross-post function to post on Twitter too.

"I appreciate a lot in this life; the things you cannot buy. Life is only once."
– Rafael Nadal

Working smartly, right? Wrong!

This essentially duplicates your Facebook post onto Twitter. It also presents problems for your audience.

Firstly, it makes it difficult for your Twitter followers to reply to your tweet. This is because (unless the Facebook post is less than 140 characters – the limit for twitter at the time of writing) those that reply to your tweet are redirected to your Facebook page in order to see the full post.

Also, assuming the Facebook post *is* more than 140 characters, Twitter truncates your tweet, which could result in your message not being understood. It may cut off your communication mid-sentence.

Additionally, Twitter's users have their own handles (for example, mine is @simonpthurston) that you may want to include in a tweet – a great way to increase engagement, by the way.

But in Facebook, you 'tag' a person or company name – a different method of engagement – so you lose the connectivity side of social media.

As a business owner, I realise that time is at a premium and that productivity hacks might seem like a good idea, but this one isn't. It's lazy and your audience will soon realise you're taking short cuts and don't have *their* best interests at heart.

Not varying or tailoring your content can also be a huge turn off for your audience. In fact 56 per cent of people say they unfollow brands because their social media content is boring.

"Captaincy is something you get better at through experience.
You've got to trust your instincts."
– Andrew Flintoff

But what *does* appeal to people?

The top three types of content consumers enjoy and respond to is:

1. Fresh or new
2. Relevant
3. Engaging

So how do you add variety into your messaging?

You could structure it so that 60 per cent of content is informative or educational, 25 per cent is shared from other posts or pages, and the remaining 15 per cent could be commercial or promotional.

Sharing others' content is perfectly fine, by the way. It also shows you have your finger on the pulse of what's going on in your industry and it will also help galvanise rapport with those whose content you're sharing.

Ditching a one-size-fits-all approach to your content doesn't mean you can't be smart about how you repurpose your content. Sometimes subtle tweaks are all that's required.

But varying your content shows you care about your audience and also enables you to add a more personalised side to it. Additionally, you can take advantage of the strengths and nuances of each platform.

For example: more often than not, videos outperform images on Facebook and Twitter in terms of engagement. However, as visual content is 40 times more likely to be shared on social media than just text, you should regularly use both.

"Nothing is work unless you'd rather be doing something else."
– George Halas

It's also important to know that hashtags are very useful when using Twitter and Instagram, to pick up on and use current trends. Hashtags are not quite as important on Facebook, and LinkedIn doesn't really support them in a user-friendly manner... yet.

To Give Is To Inspire

Although you may not yet know it yet, you have a wealth of amazing content that you could be using across social media. Event highlights, tips, advice, insights, a behind the scenes look at your brand, your team and you.

All of this can be used to help humanise your brand, drive differentiation and create engagement. The possibilities are limitless.

We hear a lot about "*adding value*" and it's something I'll mention time and again in this book, because it really is very important. But what exactly does it mean?

One huge asset you can use is to share your insights with your audience. And don't be afraid that you may be giving away trade secrets for free.

By doing so, you'll be pleasantly surprised at how many people will seek you out as an expert.

Your journey, interests, opinions and advice could all help, motivate, encourage or inspire people. Don't be afraid to put yourself out there.

You'll also want to find that sweet spot between posting too little and posting too much. If you have enough content to produce five posts per day, week in and week out, then do it.

"We create success or failure on the course primarily by our thoughts."
– Gary Player

It's different for each business, but ultimately it's about consistency. So some planning is needed but it's not as difficult as you might believe.

The prize for understanding this is a loyal following. It's the difference between a company that only promotes itself and one that cares about its audience, shares common interests, delivers value and isn't pushy.

As well as providing ideal platforms to communicate, many forget it also offers perhaps an even more important advantage. The ability to listen.

By monitoring your social channels, you can ensure you're not missing meaningful conversations across the web.

These days there are many platforms and apps – such as Hootsuite and Tweetdeck – that allow you to listen in on conversations across Facebook, Twitter and elsewhere.

Social listening data can provide you with valuable insights. You'll be able to quickly spot trends, find out what your audience is talking about, identify new competitors and find key influencers in your industry.

You can also track opinions on your own brand, products and services.

"Winners, I am convinced, imagine their dreams first. They want it with all their heart and expect it to come true. There is, I believe, no other way to live."
– Joe Montana

Big Data. Big Opportunities

Each time someone clicks like, share or comments on a post, they leave a data trail. This can give you valuable insights about their preferences, actions, interests and what they like to buy.

Although this type of data mining might seem a little too technical, it *should* be part of your strategy.

If you and your team aren't comfortable doing it, hire someone – even if it's short term. It's definitely worth it.

Information that uncovers your audience's likes and dislikes, type of promotions they respond to and content they enjoy is absolutely invaluable to you.

Also be mindful that the effectiveness of the data you're gathering is only as good as the goals you've set out. Think about what it is it you want to achieve and align your data to those objectives.

Ask yourself questions such as: what type of data is most beneficial to your business? How could it be applied? Who exactly is your target audience? The key is to be as specific as possible.

The good new is, you don't need to create a long list of objectives – keep them simple.

It may be that you want to deliver valuable video content that drives viewers to your YouTube channel.

"Today, you have 100% of your life left."
– Tom Landry

Perhaps you want to interview well-known personalities in your niche on Facebook Live and drive interest, engagement and credibility. Maybe you want to point people in the direction of super helpful blog posts you've written?

Or you may have a special offer you want to promote to increase sales by a minimum of 10 per cent next month.

Once you define them, you can work back from these objectives. How can you create stories that engage, excite and inspire and ultimately lead to your goal?

How can you deliver so much value that eventually your offer will be impossible to resist?

You have to have an end goal in mind. Not doing so is like walking into a gym and using the first piece of equipment you see without changing the settings the previous person was using.

Single Out Your Audience With Laser-Like Precision

In the digital revolution, advertising doesn't need to be like using a shotgun any more. No more spraying bullets around and seeing what you hit. It's time to bring out a sniper rifle and zero in on your audience with absolute precision.

This is yet another game-changer for small and medium sized businesses. With social media advertising, you can reach your target audience with greater accuracy and more cheaply than many traditional avenues, such as TV, radio, billboards and magazines.

"I think self-awareness is probably the most important thing towards being a champion."
– Billie Jean King

Facebook in particular, has a selection of sophisticated and extensive targeting options. It knows a lot about your audience: their location, birthday, age, gender, friends and interests.

Pretty much everything that Facebook knows about your audience can be used for targeting purposes on their advertising platform. Just think about how powerful that is.

If you're a sporting goods retail outlet in Manchester, you can target by geography. This ensures that only those who are within a realistic commuting distance of your store will see your advert. You're not wasting valuable advertising budget.

What if you own a gymnasium? Why not target those who have liked Facebook pages related to bodybuilding, running, and nutrition. This is how specific you can be with your targeting.

One reason I like Facebook ads is they blend nicely into your timeline. Other than the word "*Sponsored*" appearing above the post, the look and feel of adverts is not dissimilar to regular posts

They don't come across as annoying, interrupting or irrelevant. Equally, they're designed to get in front of the right sets of eyeballs. This is almost unheard of in traditional advertising.

Another area where Facebook ads empower your audience is by giving them choices.

"Today I will do what others won't, so tomorrow I can accomplish what others can't."
– Jerry Rice

Click on the three dots in the top right-hand corner, and they can see why they're being shown that particular ad, or they can mute it altogether. How's that for user experience?

This is the antithesis of the annoying pop ups you encounter on some websites. You try to click on the 'x' to cancel the pop up, but it's deliberately designed to be either too small or very hard to see.

P*** your audience off once and you lose them for good.

Facebook also helps you by giving you a selection of calls to action to use for your adverts. You may want test different approaches – perhaps seeing which works best out of "*Sign Up*" and "*Learn More.*" These are just two of the options currently available.

Finally, Facebook ads are relatively inexpensive. You could certainly run an ad for one day for a paltry £10.

And by targeting effectively, you could potentially reach a thousand or more people with that small investment.

Just consider how much an advert in your local newspaper or trade magazine would cost. And how targeted it would be.

"It has been a long journey, but if you dream and have the ambition and want to work hard, then you can achieve."
– Sir Mo Farah

This alone emphasises the power of precision advertising in the digital revolution. Today, you have the ability to reach a significant number of people – all for the price of a couple of cappuccinos from your favourite coffee shop.

Once again, Facebook is only one option. But if you're quite new or relatively inexperienced when it comes to social media, it's a good place to start.

Plus, the targeting and reach their advertising can achieve are perfect when first getting started.

Whilst social media can be used successfully without ever having to personally meet anyone, the key is to be human. If you're authentic, polite, responsive and helpful, you won't go far wrong, as long as your activity is consistent and productive.

Engagement is where the magic is – creating relevant, useful, interesting and sharable content. Once you master this, there's no need to rely on uninspired, interruptive broadcasts.

You'll attract interaction, create engagement, people will share your messages, and they'll recommend you to others. As a result, your brand and communications will be amplified across the social networks you operate on.

In addition, you'll start to identify those companies that *are* simply broadcasting sales messages with the majority of their output. You'll know which ones are doing it right and which ones are not.

And you'll realise just how far you've come in your social media journey.

> *"Every disadvantage has its advantage."*
> – Johan Cruyff

TAKE A TIMEOUT!

Spend the next 10 minutes or so thinking about how you can use social media to enhance your visibility and grow your reach.

Who exactly is your target audience?

On which platforms are they spending the most time?

If you're currently using social media, how often are you posting?

Notes:

"Remember all things are possible for those who believe."
– Gail Devers

You Are Who Google Says You Are

Want to find a gym in Tottenham? Google can tell you. Need a sports physiotherapist in Cheltenham? Google knows.

Looking for an online sports nutrition store that delivers the next day? Try Google. Keen to connect with other sports clubs in the UK? You know where to look.

So, how can *you* use this to your advantage?

You need to be visible... very visible. Your website, blog, Facebook page, YouTube channel, Twitter account and Instagram page. Any digital touch point that you have should be used with care, strategic consideration and to its absolute maximum potential.

In this fast-paced, digital world, information is only a few seconds away. When considering using or buying a product or service, most people head for Google first before making contact – even if they've been referred by someone they trust.

Google has become the go-to resource for most people to research, validate and discover. From delving into their family history and finding out the winners of the 1981 FA Cup Final – to baby name ideas and recommendations for hotels in Marbella.

In fact Google processes more than 220 million searches per hour.

It's used so much, it even entered the Oxford English dictionary as a verb: to google!

"Every day is not perfect."
– Brett Favre

Your reputation is now largely defined by what shows up online. And the results of those searches will greatly determine whether or not you receive a call, email, website visit or walk-in customer.

This places great pressure and importance on your website. How easy is it for people to find it? Does it quickly and clearly communicate your expertise and value? Is it enhancing your differentiation, trust factor and reputation?

And as we discussed in the last chapter, your social media presence plays a part, too. Are you helpful, polite and approachable?

It's not always about what you say, but about what others say about you. First impressions count online, too.

People will find you online through a variety of sources. It might be a page on your site that focuses on a particular challenge they're facing.

Perhaps it's expert insights delivered through articles you've written, or an interesting YouTube video. They may have even stumbled upon a tweet that answered a specific question relevant to them.

Therefore, you must ensure you publish content online that not only presents your ideas and solutions, but your true values and beliefs.

You must be your authentic self, because you are who Google says you are.

"Everything negative – pressure, challenges – is all an opportunity for me to rise."
– Kobe Bryant

In the digital revolution, your brand is constantly under a microscope. Many believe a company's brand relates to its logo and visual image, but in reality it's so much more than that.

It's your messages, customer experience, products and services. It's your values and purpose and people's perceptions of you. Even the way you answer the phone, and respond to emails and tweets. It's the glue that binds your business.

Are You A Superhero?

As my business partner James so eloquently puts it, there's a story element too, which also helps your audience connect and align with your brand:

"A business without a strong brand is like Batman without the car, utility belt, suit, cape, cowl and more importantly – the hero's story."

"Without all of the elements that support the Batman brand – you're left with an average Joe walking around with a bat obsession."

Adding the all-important story aspect to your brand allows your audience to understand you, relate to you and become loyal to you. Look at any great brand – they all have a story at their core. It's often written into their mission or vision.

"Difficulties in life are intended to make us better, not bitter."
– Dan Reeves

Without a story, your audience won't understand your true purpose, why you're different and may instead become brand advocates for your competition.

A high quality, brand image is integral to elevating your credibility, authenticity and positioning in your industry. It's like a spotlight shining down on your business.

A great place to start is to think about *why* you started the business. I'm pretty sure it's not just about earning a living, right?

And when it comes to your brand, it's crucial to have consistency across your entire landscape of touch points.

The tone, look and feel of your website should be aligned to your social media. These should in turn match the experience your customers have when they speak to or meet you and your staff face-to-face.

Congruency is the driving force that underpins your brand values. People are intrigued by what you do, why you do what you do, and how you do what you do.

This can and should be built into your story. It gives your audience a crystal clear understanding about you and why you're doing this. It shows them this is more than just a business to you – it's more than just about the money.

Do this well, and it builds greater trust and demonstrates authenticity and transparency in you and your brand.

"As you walk down the fairway of life you must smell the roses,
for you only get to play one round."
– Ben Hogan

Think about why *you* choose to engage with or buy certain brands and what you feel by doing so. What is it that appeals to you? Is it about *what* they do or *why* and *how* they do it?

Apple is of course one of the most iconic brands on the planet, and perhaps the best example of a brand that has almost cult-like appeal. Their stores, devices and adverts all deliver the same renowned Apple experience.

What about Nike, Amazon, Starbucks, Emirates, Rolex and Ferrari? What brands do you gravitate towards... and why?

It's Not Just For The Big Boys

You may well be thinking that whilst they're great role models for how a brand should be positioned, they're also multi-billion pound global corporations. And so how does that affect you, as a small business owner or emerging brand?

While that's true, so are the overriding principles. Once you clearly and consistently demonstrate your brand values across every platform, you become more trusted and valuable in your industry.

Your brand values are your true magnetic north. They're your philosophy, culture, vision and values. They're the heart and soul of your business.

When consumers commit to buying from you, they aren't just investing in a product or service – they're investing in what your brand stands for. People buy on emotion and justify it with logic – so you need to make that emotional connection with them.

"Persistence can change failure into extraordinary achievement."
– Matt Biondi

One way to engage the right emotions with your audience is making them feel like they know your brand and they can trust you. That's why it's so important to design your brand around your authentic self.

It also ensures consistency, because you're not trying to be something or someone you're not.

Delivering brand consistency is part of building trust with your audience. When people know you, they'll relate to you and your purpose.

And when people feel like they know and trust you, they're more likely to buy from you, be loyal to you – and recommend you.

Be confident, bold, transparent and true to your purpose. Then be sure to share this across your marketing communications and touch points.

Your Most Important Brand Ambassadors

And it's not just about ensuring your clients and prospects are clear on your brand's personality and values. You have potential brand ambassadors right under your nose.

Think of the positive impact cultivating a clear, consistent and distinctive brand-led culture could have on your business.

Imagine your staff – and any contractors you have working with you – being fully engaged with your brand and mission.

*"You are never really playing an opponent. You are playing
yourself, your own highest standards."*
– Arthur Ashe

When individuals genuinely feel a part of something special, something with purpose, they are more productive, creative and motivated.

They know the distinct ways you create value for your clients off by heart and understand why you're different from your competitors.

Suddenly, money isn't the be-all and end-all. Your team is far more likely to stay loyal to you for what you do, how you do it and how you make them feel. They thrive and feel happy in a vibrant culture, and are proud to tell others that they work for or with you.

This is the power of a great brand and it's easier to do than you might think – but it does take a little time, thought and application.

When you employ new staff or bring on board new partners, it's a good idea to immerse them in your company's brand immediately. You could create a mini handbook or a simple onboarding welcome pack.

Ensure all communications prior to and once they join reflect your brand. This is actually a great way to pre-screen potential staff and partners. If they don't 'get' your brand, they're probably not right for you.

For those that are, the payoff is a team that is totally aligned to your cause and understands your brand inside and out. When telling their friends and family, they'll use words that you would use, highlight your USPs with clarity and do it with genuine enthusiasm.

"The ones who want to achieve and win championships motivate themselves."
– Mike Ditka

If you have or decide to bring marketing communications in-house, your team will know exactly the words to use to describe your business and its activity. They'll also be able to brief agencies on the same – freeing up yet more of your time.

Your team is the epicentre of your brand. Every day they're literally living and breathing it. In the digital revolution, where information is abundant and reviews are widespread, employees are your de facto brand ambassadors.

The essence of your brand is integral to the growth and success of your business. It is also dictated by how those closest to it embody, represent and embrace it.

That includes you.

TAKE A TIMEOUT!

Spend 10 minutes thinking about your values – both personal and business.

What words describe how you want your customers to feel?

What dreams and goals do you have for your business?

What words are aligned to your own personal values?

Notes:

"Nobody who ever gave his best regretted it."
– George Halas

The World Is Full Of Great Ideas, But...

My wife Kerrie is super creative. She's worked in multiple industries from luxury jewellery and lingerie to healthcare and interior design. She's held a variety of managerial roles in several countries around the world.

Kerrie has that creative spark and ability to think outside the box. She's had ideas before products ever appeared in retail outlets. One day, she covered her Sony Ericsson mobile phone in small stick-on faux crystals. A few years later, crystal bling mobile phone covers were all the rage, and are still popular today.

We fly quite a lot. When our daughter Daisy was a baby, my wife quickly realised that trying to get her comfortable and sleep onboard a plane was no easy feat.

So she explained to me her idea of a cushioned type of bed that would strap to the back of the seat in front. It would provide a long, flat platform from the child's seat to the one in front, so that any little one could stretch out more comfortably and eventually go to sleep.

And then around 18 months later, I noticed the launch of a new product called Fly Legs Up. It's the brainchild of three Australian women who had encountered exactly the same challenge that we had.

So how much are ideas worth?

My wife's ideas, my ideas and your ideas are worth nothing without execution.

"Never let the fear of striking out get in your way."
– Babe Ruth

They're great to have, but can't be bought or sold. They have no intrinsic value. To receive any kind of value, you have to implement.

This is an area where business owners struggle the most. Very few actually take action and execute their ideas – while those that do, aren't always sure how to execute properly.

In a moment I'll discuss how you can take your implementation and execution to a new level. Before I do, let's quickly look at a very famous example that illustrates the power of effective execution.

A Story About Bill And Steve

If I asked 100 people which company was the first to bring the modern day tablet PC to market, I'm pretty sure most would say Apple, with their iPad.

But there's an interesting twist to this story, and it doesn't involve Steve Jobs, but his longtime friend, foe and at one time business ally, Bill Gates.

Microsoft had been conducting some new research. They discovered people wanted the convenience of a smaller, portable PC, but with the same capabilities as a desktop or laptop.

So in 2002 they developed the Microsoft Tablet PC – something Gates famously predicted would be the most popular form of PC sold in America.

This was a full eight years before Apple would unleash their first generation iPad on to the world stage.

"The first 90 minutes of a football match are the most important."
– Sir Bobby Robson

So the demand was there and as we now know, it would be a decade before their nearest competitor followed suit.

But I don't know anyone who owns a Microsoft Tablet PC. Do you?

So what happened?

Microsoft believed the tablet should have the same hardware as a fully loaded PC and equipped it accordingly. But this was like installing a Ferrari engine into a BMW – both were high spec pieces of kit, but weren't completely compatible.

The touchscreen was poorly developed and used a stylus, making it awkward to use.

Also, the price tag was as fully loaded as the hardware, coming in at a cool £1,500. And don't forget, this was in 2002.

Steve Jobs recognised a tablet was more of a playful, consumer device and not simply a direct replacement for a desktop or laptop.

He knew a streamlined operating system would be perfect and that his BMW would not need a Ferrari engine.

Jobs also understood that to create something different, you need to think differently. In fact that philosophy also inspired one of Apple's advertising slogans in the late 1990s.

"To finish first, you must first finish."
– Rick Mears

And so on January 27th 2010, Apple announced the launch of their revolutionary device, with a price point of around £400 – almost a quarter of the price of the Microsoft machine.

So, how can you transfer your ideas into a tangible action plan?

Think about your objectives and write down your end goal(s) and the result(s) you want to achieve. Decide *realistically* how long you believe they will take.

Hint: this will generally be shorter than you think. Don't let procrastination slow you down.

Then, plug those activities into your schedule and commit to doing them. I guarantee working consistently each day will skyrocket your productivity.

And don't feel you have to do this on your own. Seek advice and help if needed.

Start by getting everything down on paper. Create a brain dump of every idea, no matter how big or small or silly or irrelevant you think it may be at this early stage.

To get your creative juices flowing, you may want to go somewhere outside your normal working environment to do this. I like to go to the park or a coffee shop. Try somewhere you wouldn't normally go and see what works for you.

If you have multiple ideas, I advise that you prioritise them based on your objectives. Are you looking for more leads and sales? Do you need to improve your branding or messaging?

"If you can't dream big, ridiculous dreams, what's the point in dreaming at all?"
– Ronda Rousey

Then for each one, you can apply this simple three-step strategy:

1. **Investigate and Imagine**

   Look at your ideas from a different, more curious perspective. Don't feel pressurised to make the idea work at this early stage.

   Try to visualise what your business will look like when the idea comes to fruition. How would it impact you, your team and your clients?

2. **Mind the Gap**

   If your idea is for a new product or service, is there a definite void in the market? Will it actually solve a real challenge that your audience has?

   And will it meet their needs in a new, remarkable way? How will you ensure it stands out and isn't lost in the noise?

3. **Congruency**

   Is there symmetry between your idea and your vision, ethos and values? Does it fit in with your long-term goals? Does it fit with your other products and services?

From there, refine some of the clearer ideas into a more structured manner. It may still be a bit haphazard at this stage, but that's ok. You're starting to filter the wheat from the chaff.

"The difference between the impossible and the possible lies in a man's determination."
– Tommy Lasorda

Continue to refine it until you have something a bit more concrete. Regardless of whether it's a product, service, initiative or campaign – think about whether you can implement all of it yourself or if you need external expertise.

Be realistic and decisive – this is no place for procrastination.

When it comes to selling the vision for your idea, simplicity is the key. Keeping it simple will help maximise interest, engagement and buy-in for your idea.

You should create a pitch for your idea. Make sure you write it down and learn it until you can recite it without reading it.

Then rehearse it with people to see if they understand your vision and to ensure it sounds natural.

Having a powerful pitch allows you to clearly communicate your message in a way that people instantly understand what you're offering. This means you must be crystal clear about the challenges you will solve, the value you have to offer and the impact you believe you will make.

Having got this down to a tee, you can now present your ideas to a company that will be able to help bring your idea to fruition. It's also useful to provide them with any reference material, images or videos to add further clarity to what you want the end result to look like.

Once you've worked on developing your new initiative, get to a stage where you feel it's pretty much ready. If it's a product or service, you should test it with a select audience, before unleashing it onto the general public.

"It's all about the journey, not the outcome."
– Carl Lewis

You could provide your prototype product or service gratis or at nominal cost. Explain that in return, you would like honest feedback on potential shortcomings, improvements, or areas that may be over-delivering.

You want the good, the bad and the ugly. That way, you can identify any improvements that are required.

Often we can't see the wood for the trees, so real-life insights from a third party are extremely valuable. This is a risk-free opportunity to eliminate any bugs, roadblocks and develop a more polished version.

The ultimate aim of your product or service is to create raving fans. Satisfied clients that are happy to talk about it to friends, family and colleagues, share it on social media and recommend you to others as a trusted supplier.

I'm sure you've stayed at a hotel, eaten at a restaurant, or used a business that provided you with a stunning experience.

An experience that afterwards, you just had to tell everyone about. And perhaps you posted photos or videos of it on social media?

That's exactly what you're looking for. Don't just settle for the ordinary – think bigger, think impact, think differently.

Once again, you may think this is only reserved for the Amazons and Apples of this world, but that couldn't be farther from the truth. We live in a time where consumers want bespoke and personalised experiences *for everything.*

"One who is persistent will excel."
– Venus Williams

This is where, as a small business – you have the upper hand. Use your size and agility to your advantage.

You must believe in yourself and just as importantly, be accountable. Many fail to bring an idea to fruition because unexpected challenges derail them and they're no longer willing to be accountable.

They may see the end result, the potential, and the impact their idea could have, but aren't willing to put in the sweat equity. They may be a matter of weeks away from bringing their idea to market, but give up at the final hurdle.

But as we've already discussed, you don't have to do this alone.

Although ideation is distinctly different to execution, there may be technical requirements or skills that you either don't have or don't have time for.

You can empower some of your team to take care of such areas. Alternatively, search for partners who can help. There is a glut of expertise out there – you just need to look or it.

The good news is that in the digital revolution, such expertise is far easier to find than it was as recently as a decade ago.

And don't put too much pressure on yourself. Yes you want to lead the project and ensure milestones are hit, but take the time to appreciate the journey.

Be patient rather than getting stressed about achieving your desired results too soon.

> *"I've got a theory that if you give 100% all of the time, somehow things will work out in the end."*
> – Larry Bird

In the next chapter, you'll discover how to get the right foundations in place to be able bring your A-game to the digital revolution. A six-step process that will sharpen your focus, clarify your vision and create a stand-out digital presence.

It's time to stop playing small and ASPIRE to grow the value you deliver, your reach and your revenue.

TAKE A TIMEOUT!

Spend 10 minutes thinking about a potential new product or service you could develop for your customers.

What type of product or service is it?

How would it transform the lives of your clients?

What's stopping you from creating this product or service?

Notes:

"If you only ever give 90% in training then you will only ever give 90% when it matters."
– Michael Owen

PART TWO

ASPIRE TO GREATNESS

Aspire

/ə'spʌɪə/

verb

To direct one's hopes or ambitions towards achieving something.
*"We never thought that we might **aspire to** those heights."*

Synonyms: desire (to), aim for/to, set one's heart on, want (to), expect (to), have the objective of, dream of, hunger for/to, seek (to), pursue, have as one's goal/aim, set one's sights on; be ambitious.

The Past Cannot Be Changed, But The Future Is In Your Power

Without a time machine or crystal ball, there's no way of predicting the future of digital. That's obvious, right?

But history gives us some pretty good clues as to what likely lies ahead. The agricultural age made way for steam power and mechanisation, which eventually evolved to electricity and mass production.

And more recently, electronics and automated production have become commonplace. Progress is undeniably constant.

"Strength does not come from winning. Your struggles develop your strengths."
– Arnold Schwarzenegger

Currently, we're only scratching the surface of possibility when it comes to digital. It's still in its infancy.

But to understand how quickly technology can evolve, let's have a quick glance at its progress during the last quarter of a century.

Sir Tim Berners-Lee and his team launched the World Wide Web in 1991, but it wasn't until 1993 that it starting to become (relatively speaking) mainstream.

By 1994 there were 16 million users worldwide, and in just 24 months this rose to 70 million. This growth would set the tone of what was to come.

As its popularity grew, so did the digital landscape. The launch of search engines Yahoo! (1994) and Google (1997) gave users a way to research and find information like never before.

Suddenly e-commerce became a thing, with Amazon and eBay joining the game. The die had been cast.

The infamous dot com bubble of the early 2000s was a massive (but necessary) bump in the road.

It weeded out companies with vastly unrealistic share prices, huge investment and little or no profit.

It was a huge wake up call, even for businesses such as Amazon, Cisco and PayPal. All three weathered the storm and thrive today.

"There's always going to be somebody who takes a dislike to you and you can't waste time worrying about it."
– Paula Radcliffe

But the crash also created several technology innovations and platforms that we now take for granted. These include instant internet access, cloud computing, social media and mobile.

And within five years, LinkedIn, Facebook and Twitter emerged and the number of global internet users topped 1.1 billion.

Once again, crisis equals opportunity.

The dot com bubble is a lesson we can all learn from. Whilst there were several factors that led to the crash, many perished because their strategies were flawed, their focus was amiss and their execution was poor.

So, how can *you* thrive in these transformational times?

Every business is unique. However, there are predictable digital challenges that hold most businesses back.

For some, it's creating the right strategy, executing effectively and articulating their value with clarity. For others, it's overcoming time and knowledge gaps, uncertainty in where to focus their efforts and understanding how to generate more leads.

And so with the experience of working with hundreds of SMEs across four continents, my team and I developed ASPIRE.

In six methodical, sequential steps, ASPIRE is designed to enhance your online visibility, amplify your business' digital footprint, drive ambitious growth and help you succeed in a digital world.

> *"Great moments are born from great opportunities."*
> – Herb Brooks

ASPIRE
Step One: Audit

Audit. Just hearing the word either strikes terror into most people or reduces them to boredom.

And while they're commonplace in financial and accounting circles, I rarely see them performed in a marketing context.

Which is odd, because if you're (quite rightly) focusing on the numbers in your business, why would you not be focusing on one of the key activities that helps drive your numbers?

Another reason an audit is beneficial is it helps you align your true business objectives to your vision. It allows you to analyse your competitors, obstacles and anticipate opportunities. It's the first critical foundation for growth.

It's where we start with every new client we work with.

How can we possibly advise on what areas are doing well, which ones need more work and identify new growth opportunities without an audit?

It would be like your doctor prescribing medication without examining you first.

"Excellence is not a singular act but a habit. You are what you do repeatedly."
– Shaquille O'Neal

This chapter will explain how an audit helps **identify goals, strengths and possible weaknesses, as well as access quick wins.**

It also gives you your very own framework template to use at any time to complete your own marketing audit.

An audit examines every aspect of a company's marketing and activities. What is your business trying to achieve? What marketing strategies are you currently using? What level of success are you enjoying?

The devil is most certainly in the detail.

The process is not overly complex but it is methodical. Working through each area in sequence ensures you don't miss anything. It provides you with new insights, ideas and inspiration that you can use in your business.

You most likely know every area the audit focuses on very well. However, with everything else going on in your business on a daily basis, you might not have actively worked on each component with the required detail.

The key is to take an impartial view and be honest with yourself. And don't be tempted to skip any of the four areas.

This process is designed to deliver **sustainable growth for your business, so the end result is more than worth it.**

If your profits are showing healthy growth, don't be complacent. If you're doing "*ok,*" don't think you can't do better.

"Knowing is not enough, we must apply. Willing is not enough, we must do."
– Bruce Lee

If business is a struggle right now, don't delay. This is an extremely valuable exercise that you should undertake at least once a year.

I'm pretty sure you now understand the importance of a marketing audit, right? So let's dive into to the four areas:

Audit: Customer Analysis

To kick this off, think about who is **already buying your products or services. Now think about who your ideal customer is.**

What if you could cherry pick from your prospects and *only* work with those that fit your archetypal criteria for a dream customer?

Who are they? What do they look like?

A great way to get crystal clear on exactly who your ideal customer is, is by creating a customer avatar. Let me explain:

In essence you create a fictional character that represents your dream customer. You give them a name, think about where they live, what car they drive and what their hobbies are.

Are they married? Where do they go on holiday? What's their occupation?

You need to have empathy. Put yourself in your customer avatar's shoes –understand who they are, what their hopes and dreams are, as well as their fears and concerns.

"When you walk up to opportunity's door: don't knock it – kick that bitch in, smile and introduce yourself"
– Dwayne Johnson

Once you've got a clear image in your head, write down (at least) three reasons why they're an ideal customer and how you help them. What value are you delivering? Why do they choose you and not your competitors?

You might think this is a waste of time, but here's why I believe it's important: if you try and speak to everyone, you end up speaking to no one.

I'm sure you'll have different age groups of prospects, for example: aged 20 to 25 and 30 to 35. Each has slightly different challenges, needs and goals.

But rather than designing your marketing communications to try and appeal to everyone, you need to narrow your focus. Tailor your messaging to your customer avatar, instead of spreading it too thinly so that it becomes diluted and ends up not appealing to anyone.

You may think by really drilling down and niching your target audience that you'll lose out on other potential customers. Those individuals that still fit your profile and are close to being dream customers.

But you'll notice that something incredible happens. Even though you're focusing on a specific avatar, you'll still attract others from outside that avatar. They will see the messaging designed for your customer avatar, and most of it will resonate with them, too.

This is because there will be overlaps in their characteristics, needs, objectives and challenges. And think about it, there are some people that although they're 19, act like they're 30. And vice-versa.

"Nobody roots for Goliath."
– Wilt Chamberlain

You may be targeting men between 25 and 30 for your martial arts school, but find that you still attract women in the same age range who have the same energy and enthusiasm for the sport. But it all came from highly tailored and focused messaging based around your customer avatar.

If you sell a wide range of products and services to different types of customers, you can create multiple avatars. Go through the exact same exercise for each, but here's some advice:

Make sure you master one first and then move onto the next. You must do them one at a time. Also, try and keep it simple. Whilst you may feel you have eight, 10 or more groups of potential customers, it's far better to specialise. Perhaps set a limit at four, at least to begin with.

Audit: Marketing Activity

More and more people are consuming and engaging with content via desktop, mobile, tablet, and across browsers and touch points. The opportunities to connect with your audience have never been more abundant.

By analysing your messaging and marketing campaigns, you can better understand what's working and what isn't. You'll understand where your strengths and weaknesses are.

And crucially, you'll get insights into what improvements are needed.

The digital revolution has disrupted the traditional sales process. Mobile phones and the instant access they bring to social media and the online world are transforming how businesses market themselves.

"To give any less than your best is to sacrifice a gift."
– Steve Prefontaine

People are glued to their phones at home, on the go and even during dinner.

Not only that, but they're multi-tasking. They're posting on social media about something they just saw on the news, on Britain's Got Talent, sporting events or their favourite Netflix series.

But here's the good news: these are factors that you can and should be taking advantage of.

So, as well as delivering products or services to your clients, you need to add another string to your bow: become a media company.

"A media company? But Simon, I'm a <insert type of company>."

And of course you're right, but let me explain.

In the highly connected and competitive digital revolution, you need to be where your audience is spending most of their time.

It's a bit like going fishing and casting your rods in all the places the fish are hanging out. But of course the fish are your target audience.

And so by becoming a media company – essentially producing a variety of content across different platforms and touch points – you're putting your company in front of as many eyeballs as possible.

"What you lack in talent can be made up with desire, hustle, and giving 110 per cent all the time."
– Don Zimmer

Regardless of how many digital assets you're using and how much content you're producing, it can seem overwhelming.

That's perfectly natural.

It's also one of the reasons I've written this book. I find the easiest way is to look at the big picture and then break it down.

Define the goals of your content. Is it educating your customer, raising awareness or communicating a special offer?

Having a clear goal helps you reverse engineer the pathway and create appropriate content for each context.

Think about your current messaging and marketing collaterals – both online and offline. How are they relevant to your customers? What type of messages are they most receptive to?

Is your messaging generating leads? How are you segmenting your messaging? What search terms do visitors use to find you online? What social media platforms are they using?

An audit is about asking a lot of quality questions to reveal a bunch of insightful answers.

Don't be afraid to become uncomfortable with the answers – this approach will elevate you above the majority of your competitors.

It will also ensure you have thorough knowledge of how you should position your content and what types of content your audience responds to.

"I always thought records were there to be broken."
– Michael Schumacher

What can be measured, can be improved. I can't understate the importance of doing this.

Audit: Competitor Analysis

We *all* have competitors – but just how well do you know and understand them?

Your primary focus should always be *your* business – where *you* are and where *you* want to go. But it's still important to understand what your competitors are doing and how you can gain an edge over them.

For the purpose of this exercise, I suggest you analyse your top three competitors. Knowing what they offer, surveying their website and researching their social media activity is a good start.

Analyse the quality and types of content they're using and how they use it. Are they blogging, writing articles, uploading videos and if so, how often? Are they educating and engaging their audience or just promoting themselves?

How many followers do they have and is there much interaction? And how many listings appear when you google their name?

However, I also suggest you dig a little deeper than this. Once again, it's critical to ask quality, probing questions.

What are their strengths – is it competitive pricing or do they target premium customers? Do they demonstrate high quality service? Are they more focused on convenience?

"Make sure your worst enemy doesn't live between your own two ears."
– Laird Hamilton

Do they carry an extensive inventory? And what about any weaknesses they may have?

If they have premises, pay them a visit. Take a look around, check out their sales and promotional materials and ask their staff questions. Is their on-site look and feel congruent with their online image?

But imagine if you went beyond the visible elements of their marketing and delved into their customer experience.

Perhaps they're surprising their customers on their birthday or other notable occasions, inviting them to educational events or introducing them to partners that can successfully add value in other areas.

This might seem like a lot of work, but the fact is it really isn't once you get going. And you might just be surprised by what you can learn about your own business by evaluating your competition.

Audit: Goal Analysis

I'm sure you know that goals (I also like to refer to them as strategic objectives) are important. Without them, your business has no real direction or means of measuring success.

Goals help you improve, grow and become more profitable. I also strongly suggest you write them down.

This is something I've already alluded to and will elaborate on in the next ASPIRE step.

"You have to expect things of yourself before you can do them."
– Michael Jordan

But how do you set and organise your goals? Are you setting goals that are actually helping your business? And how often do you review your progress against them?

It's great to dream and have a big, ambitious goal, but be careful. If the distance between where you are now and where you want to be is too vast, it can overwhelm and demotivate.

And this can lead to procrastination and inertia.

I believe a goal should be a clear statement of an intended outcome you want to achieve. It should also have a timeframe, so you can formulate a plan to hit it.

By doing so, you'll be clear about exactly what you need to do and by when.

For example, it may be that you want to become a go-to expert in your industry in two year's time. Or you want to open a new outlet in another town or city within the next 12 months. Make it definite, realistic and something you can visualise and focus on.

Setting strong, clearly defined strategic objectives allows you to break them down into daily, weekly or monthly milestones.

Suddenly a goal that may seem akin to climbing Mount Everest can be achieved through consistent, cumulative action.

"I need to worry about the things that I am in control of."
– Brian O'Driscoll

It's all about a change of mindset and how you perceive the challenge that awaits you. You can either make it work for you, or against you.

I like to break my goals down into weekly activities, so that they set the majority of my schedule for the week.

Then, at the end of each week, I review my progress and if necessary, adjust my goals for the upcoming week.

It's a good idea to set some time aside at a specific time each week (perhaps Friday at 6pm) to do this. That way, it's in the calendar and you shouldn't feel tempted to push it back or ignore it.

It's *that* important.

Of course, it may take some time to get used to it. Most businesses I know don't set goals, let alone allocate time on a regular basis to assess whether they're on target or not.

This may seem like *just another* administrative task that you want to just get out of the way. But this can really transform your business.

There's another reason having and reviewing goals works. It ensures that every week, you have clear action steps mapped out that are designed to get you closer to achieving your ultimate objective(s).

In fact, before I start any ad-hoc task, one of the questions I ask myself is *"is this driving me closer to achieving any of my goals?"*

> *"Show me a guy who's afraid to look bad, and I'll show you a guy you can beat every time."*
> – Lou Brock

If it isn't, I'll assess it further as to when I should do it, whether I should delegate it or not do it at all.

And of course your goals can cover a variety of areas. The most popular tend to be growth or profit-related, focusing on increasing customers, sales, expansion and launching new products and services.

But enhancing your service could be another. Whether it's improving customer satisfaction, retention or creating raving fans that become brand advocates.

Just remember, be specific, be clear on how you can achieve them and set a realistic timeline.

There are other areas you may also want to consider. What about social goals? You may commit to giving back to the community through philanthropy or charity initiatives. In one of my businesses, we donate a percentage of revenue to two different charities.

In terms of team development, I believe individual goals are a must. By creating and monitoring targets, you can provide your team with real-time input on their performance while motivating them to achieve more.

And here's a top tip: once a goal has been set for a team member, ask *them* to explain how they plan to achieve it. This works for two reasons:

Firstly, you're empowering them and will get true insights into whether they genuinely understand your vision and goals. You'll find out a lot about them just by doing this.

"When you have confidence, you can have a lot of fun. And when you have fun, you can do amazing things."
– Joe Namath

Secondly, they may come up with some great ideas. Ideas you may not have considered. You're also instilling a culture of trust and collaboration – one that will serve you well for years to come.

For goals to be meaningful and effective in motivating your team, they should be linked to your vision and ambitions.

Employees who aren't clear on the roles they play in the success of your business are less likely to be engaged. They'll just feel as if they're *doing a job*, rather than being part of something.

Share the bigger picture you have for your business with every member of your team. Let them know what difference you want to make to the community, population or industry.

Of course, there's always sensitive information you can't share. But be honest with your team about where you want the business to be in two to five years' time.

But perhaps most important of all is having a system that empowers and motivates you and your team to achieve your goals, rather than overwhelming. Mindset plays such a key role in having the perseverance to keep going.

In Step Two, I am going to share with you the exact system I use that allows me to stay upbeat, enthusiastic and committed for the long haul.

"Once you learn to quit, it becomes a habit."
– Vince Lombardi

A S P I R E
Step Two: Strategy

Although I'm neither American nor particularly into politics, there's a quote from former US President Dwight D. Eisenhower that really resonates with me:

"In preparing for battle I have always found that plans are useless, but planning is indispensable."

I'm sure you've encountered situations that came out of left field that were never part of your business plan. Of course, stuff happens – and generally when we least expect it.

You can't possibly plan ahead for *every* eventuality. But it doesn't mean you shouldn't have a plan to try and get your business from where it is currently to where you want it to be.

As I've already mentioned, the more specific you are, the better. It helps you to plan, visualise and define objectives and activities to make it happen.

And you wouldn't go to the airport and ask for *"a ticket to anywhere but not here, please,"* would you? You need to have an idea where you want to go.

And so it is with your business. You *must* have a strategy, no matter how basic.

It's about formulating your game plan and specifying your goals and target audience. Without a sound strategy or any idea of your goals or a clear vision for your business, you're essentially on a ship that's drifting along without a compass.

"It's hard to beat a person who never gives up."
– Babe Ruth

Yes, the current may take you somewhere great like a tropical island, but you're just as likely to end up hitting a reef and capsizing. Is that really a chance you want to take?

When was the last time you thought about where you would like your business to be in 12 months, two years or five years' time? What difference would it make to your customers and the additional value you can give to them?

And what difference would it make to you, your lifestyle and your family? This is your chance to crystalise your vision and create a framework to help you reach it.

I briefly touched on this in the previous step and we'll cover goals in more detail later in this step. But now we're going to discuss the elements that will help you to achieve your goals: tactics and strategy.

Strategy vs Tactics

"Strategy without tactics is the slowest route to victory. Tactics without strategy is the noise before defeat." - Sun Tzu.

A Chinese military general, strategist and philosopher who lived over 2,000 years ago, Sun Tzu often wrote about strategy. He's perhaps most well known for his book *The Art of War.*

A lot of the wisdom he shares is applicable today, particularly in business and sports. To fully appreciate what Sun Tzu is saying, let's look at the difference between tactics and strategy.

And to illustrate this, I'll use a chess analogy.

"I never worry about the problem. I worry about the solution."
– Shaquille O'Neal

Tactics are the pieces on the chessboard – your pawns, knights, rooks and bishops – and can be deployed accordingly.

In business terms, they're your website, brochures, videos, social media channels and business cards – your collaterals.

Strategy is the *why* and *how* you use these pieces to get the maximum return on your efforts to achieve specific goals.

Like a Grandmaster, good strategic business owners play several moves ahead. They're able to anticipate, helping eliminate some of those left field challenges.

We discussed the importance of goal analysis in Step One. But being clear on the difference between tactics and strategy will help you implement your goals.

Being strategic is being clear on your objectives and the actions required to achieve them. These may include the video series you're planning, the tradeshow you're attending next quarter, and how you aim to attract and retain loyal clients.

For example: one of your strategic objectives for your website may be to position yourself as an expert in your industry. Or perhaps you want to generate subscribers to your newsletter?

By doing a little planning in advance, imagine the impact this could have on how you design your site and write your content. In fact it will totally change the way you do many things.

"What do you do with a mistake: recognise it, admit it, learn from it, forget it."
– Dean Smith

Most websites are used tactically, instead of strategically. Having great quality content and hoping the site delivers leads and sales is not a strategy.

You have to plan in advance. As the saying goes: form follows function.

Some strategic objectives you may have or want to consider:

- Positioning yourself as an expert in your sector
- Building customer loyalty
- Differentiating yourself from your competitors
- Providing high quality free information
- Gaining subscribers to your newsletter or video series
- Generating referrals
- Attracting dream clients

Setting Strategic Objectives

As I alluded to in Step One, writing goals down and understanding what you want to achieve is just as important as defining them – perhaps more so.

Humans are very visually oriented – we need to keep seeing something to stay focused on it long term.

And it doesn't actually start with your goals, but your *why*. Why are you in business? Why is this important to you?

Thinking about your why will serve as the key underlying driver in everything you do.

"All those who are around me are the bridge to my success, so they are all important."
– Manny Pacquiao

Once you've defined your why, you can then be clear on your goals. Whether it's to generate an extra 50 per cent revenue in the next 12 months, bring 150 new members on board, attend two events on behalf of your chosen charity, organise a community initiative or something else.

But this is where it gets interesting. Having established my goals, ensuring I'm absolutely clear on them, I set them to one side. I then focus on the activity that will help me reach them.

Think about it this way: if your goal is to write a book, your activity is a daily writing schedule. If your goal is to run a marathon, your activity is a daily training routine. If your goal is to attract 20 new customers next month, your activity is contacting 25 prospects/lapsed customers/leads per day for a month.

I find this system works and creates the right mindset, because the focus is on the activity, not the outcome. As long as you do the activity, you're always making progress.

The flip side is that if you focus on the goal, it can create a negative mindset if the results don't happen immediately.

And in truth, if results do happen immediately, your goals probably aren't challenging enough.

We often place unnecessary stress on ourselves to succeed in business and life: generate more sales, earn more profit, eat healthier, run faster or lose weight.

Instead, why not keep things simple by focusing on the daily activities and rigorously stick to your schedule?

"Strategy requires thought, tactics require observation."
– Machgielis "Max" Euwe

Stress and frustration are caused by lack of control. When you are fixated on a goal, you have no control over external circumstances or situations that may arise. But you *can* control your activity.

Goals are great for *planning* your progress. Your activity helps you *make* progress. Focus on your activity and watch your productivity and progress soar.

Why Choose You?

Times have changed. In any given niche (with a few exceptions), most companies provide pretty much the same types of products and services. And being good at what you do – while it helps – isn't enough any more.

In a crowded market where competition is fierce and profit margins are thin, you need to differentiate yourself.

And I'm sure you've noticed I've continually banged this drum to this point in this book. I'm unapologetic because that's how crucial it is.

By applying a more strategic approach, you'll be able to outthink your competitors. You'll also be able to **create high demand for your products and services without having to chase every sale.**

Very often this means changing long-standing business beliefs and processes that may have been in place for several years.

But the digital revolution is always evolving.

"Aim for the sky and you'll reach the ceiling. Aim for the ceiling and you'll stay on the floor."
– Bill Shankly

A new approach can reposition your business, generate greater interest and help you become more influential in your industry. By doing so, you'll also attract more opportunities and enjoy the process.

Some questions for you to consider that will help you differentiate yourself:

Are You Working With Dream Clients?

Every business has its ideal client that perfectly fits the right profile.

If you're not working with or attracting dream customers (or the numbers you'd like), it may be for a number of reasons.

Have you clearly identified exactly who they are? Start by creating an avatar and identifying the factors highlighted in Step One. Also, think about what you're offering now and what (if budget was no object) you *really* want to offer.

Are you trying to be all things to everyone so that you don't miss out on any opportunities? It's very easy to get into the habit of not turning down business and wanting to help everyone.

This can often involve offering discounts to undercut your competitors, or trying to accommodate everyone so you attract as much business as possible.

If you're currently doing this, I highly recommend you stop – now.

"Nothing good ever comes from worrying or sitting there feeling sorry for yourself. Keep positive and keep pushing on and things will turn good."
– Conor McGregor

How Do You Answer The Question *"What Do You Do?"*

Perhaps you have your own football academy, gym, or martial arts school? You may sell sports apparel, nutrition, supplements or leisurewear. Whatever it is you do, you need to communicate it in a (more) remarkable way.

Once you've determined your ideal market or sector, you can begin to articulate what you do in a different way.

With a little thought, you'll be able to create a powerful pitch that lights people up. A passionate pitch that you can't help deliver with enthusiasm that naturally leads to the listener asking the question "Tell me more about how you do that."

So are you a personal trainer or do you *"transform the physiques of men and women over 30 in 12 weeks or less?"* It's a bit more compelling, right?

What If You Focused On High-End Instead Of Time-For-Money?

You, Sir Richard Branson and I all have one thing in common: we all only have 24 hours available to us in a day. Time is the most important asset any business has.

Although time is free, you can't own it. Although you can't keep it, you can spend it. And once you've lost it, you can never get it back.

Therefore, even if you have a large team, charging by the hour will always limit you. It will limit the value you can deliver to your clients and the revenue you can generate. It's a vicious circle.

"Don't count the days; make the days count."
– Muhammad Ali

Have you considered offering high-end services or packages, instead of an hourly rate? Even though it may be 'the norm' in your industry, why not group five coaching sessions (for example) into a package? Or offer a residential course?

Investigate ways in which you can bundle products and services together and at the same time deliver additional value. How can you structure your product or service range to attract a different calibre of customer?

What If You Created (More) Partnerships?

A partnership (also known as a strategic alliance or joint venture) is a powerful way to grow your revenue by leveraging your existing value with others.

By partnering with a non-competing business, you can transform your business and take it to a whole new level.

One of the key elements of a successful partnership is that it should create a win/win for you and the other company, as well as the customer. But where can you find potential partners?

They may be one of your existing customers or suppliers. Why not look at networking events or tradeshows?

You may have even come across a Facebook or Google ad for a company that has partnership potential. Keep your eyes and ears open – there are opportunities everywhere.

"Never underestimate the power of dreams and the influence of the human spirit. We are all the same in this notion: The potential for greatness lives within each of us."
– Wilma Rudolph

Partnerships are one of the fastest ways to access new customers, new markets and even new industries. I'll go into more detail about how you can leverage the power of partnerships in Part Three.

What If You Published (More) Content?

In the digital revolution, there are numerous ways and channels to publish content. Blogs, articles, whitepapers, videos, podcasts – all can be leveraged cheaply and easily.

Publishing more content helps position you as a credible authority in your industry.

Have you thought about writing a book? This is one of the most impactful ways to enhance your reputation and be seen as a go-to expert in your industry.

It may seem daunting at first, but it's ultimately about crystalising your ideas and insights into a logical format. This allows you to get your messages in front of more of your audience.

Finalising Your Strategy

Now we come to the heart and soul of your strategy. You know what your goals are, who your competitors are, who your ideal customers are and the importance of differentiating yourself.

"A champion is someone who gets up when he can't."
– Jack Dempsey

It's time finalise and set your communications plan in motion.

A great marketing strategy targets your audience at every stage of your sales cycle. It delivers messages that appeal to, engage with, educate and entertain your audience. It understands that it's a marathon, not a sprint.

You must ensure you create compelling, eye-catching content that instantly grabs attention. Think about how people use social media: they scroll through their feeds at 100 miles per hour, particularly when on their phones.

You have two to three seconds to hook them in and read, watch or click.

So for the most part, you must focus on simple, concise copy that gets to the point quickly or distinctive visuals that stand out or surprise your audience.

Emails are still effective and give you the chance to say more. However, it doesn't mean that you should drone on and on.

Keep it punchy and interesting – but don't be afraid to tell the entire story.

The very fact you have someone's email address is often a good indication they are interested in what you've got to say. People don't often give their email address unwillingly, so build upon on that.

You can also direct them to your YouTube channel or blog during an email. That way, the email doesn't need to be long and they become more familiar with your other digital assets.

"Run when you can, walk if you have to, crawl if you must – just never give up."
– Dean Karnazes

My advice: don't try and create multiple assets simultaneously – work on getting one or two (perhaps Facebook and YouTube) producing consistent content first. Once you've mastered this, you can then grow your footprint.

When you reach this stage, you're in a position to achieve what Daniel Priestley calls 7/11/4.

This refers to having someone engage with your content for **seven** hours, across **11** interactions (watching a video, reading a blog or social media post, meeting you or your staff), in **four** different locations (YouTube, Facebook, website, email, etc).

This approach can help you shorten your sales cycle and become more well known, liked and trusted in your industry.

It can also further serve to differentiate you from your competitors.

And it's worth repeating from earlier: every business *must* become a media business. You have to be producing consistent content every day across different digital assets.

In the digital revolution, you have to earn a high degree of trust in order for people to buy from you. People are more skeptical today than they've ever been.

If you work smartly – and you should, you can pre-prepare content in advance. Plan ahead and perhaps dedicate three or four days a month specifically for this purpose.

"If you don't believe in yourself how will somebody else believe in you?"
– Deion Sanders

In addition, always be aware of opportunities to video or capture moments that you can use. Encourage your team to do likewise.

With a smartphone, everyone can be a content creator – so empower your employees to be on the lookout for anything that might educate, entertain or be useful to your audience.

By planning and structuring your content creation process, you don't necessarily have to physically do it every day.

And the more you do it, the better and more creative you will become.

You'll also spot more opportunities more often. It'll be effortless.

And although this process can be accelerated using the ASPIRE process, it still takes a little time – so be patient.

Going in too aggressively or not producing enough appropriate content can kill any engagement potential.

Nothing worth having comes easy and nothing valuable ever comes fast. I believe in giving more than I take – both as a human being and as a business.

Many businesses fail in the digital revolution because they don't understand how it differs from its predecessors.

It's not about who shouts loudest any more. It's about giving... and lots of it.

> *"The man who complains about the way the ball bounces is likely the one who dropped it."*
> – Lou Holtz

But by showing up every day and delivering value, you'll earn the privilege of people's attention.

I can almost guarantee that less than five per cent of your competition will be doing any of this, so it's there for the taking.

And now that your strategy is all set – it's time to test its effectiveness. Let's move onto the next step in the ASPIRE process.

"Mental will is a muscle that needs exercise, just like muscles of the body."
– Lynn Jennings

A S P I R E
Step Three: Pilot

I'm sure you've heard the saying *"practice makes perfect."* But I'm here to tell you that it doesn't.

It can create an environment where mistakes are acceptable, that it doesn't require 100 per cent focus or effort – all because it's *just* a practice. It eliminates opportunity, accountability and responsibility.

This is actually something that was drummed into me by one of the most influential sports coaches I ever had the pleasure to work with: Stewart Martyn – the former Cheltenham Town FC goalkeeping coach.

Training sessions were at a high tempo – to simulate match conditions. I'd worked hard to become a pretty good player, but under Stewart, my game grew beyond even my own expectations. I'll always be so very grateful for what he did for me.

Of course, mistakes happen and failures occur.

It's unrealistic to believe every lead will become a customer, regardless of how amazing your product or service is.

"I have never tried to compare myself to anyone else."
– Sachin Tendulkar

For some people it's the wrong time or they may not be sure; for others it may not offer exactly what they're looking for.

If you're not testing different strategies and tactics or seeking to understand why members didn't join and customers didn't buy, you're not even practicing. You're pouring money down the drain.

Which is why I use a different saying: *"perfect practice makes perfect."*

"Ok, fair enough" you might say, but what is a pilot anyway? It's simply a small-scale test-run that delivers valuable intelligence and allows you to perfect your strategy in a semi-controlled, yet real-life environment.

A pilot enables you to test different styles of messaging, imagery and types of offers to different audiences. It also helps identify strengths and weaknesses, as well as pinpoint areas for growth and diversification.

You will become clear on how to prioritise deliverables to achieve your goals.

When working with a client, we structure a pilot program with a three-step process: objectives, scope and resources.

Pilot: Objectives

This is no different to setting definitive goals for your business. And although it is (just) a pilot, you should still approach it with the same conviction, strategic mindset and commitment that you would for a full strategy rollout.

"I don't know any other way to lead but by example."
– Don Shula

Think about what you are trying to achieve and how you will define success. Do you want to increase engagement, enquiries or brand awareness? Perhaps you want to attract potential partnership or investment opportunities?

What is the end goal? If you have multiple goals, break them down. What results will you be pleased with? What do you want to learn from this pilot?

I am a big believer that there are no failures, just learning experiences. There is a vault of valuable insights to be gained from implementing a pilot – even if you don't achieve the results you're after.

Always keep an open mind and be willing to learn from the experience. It does move you forward towards achieving your overall objectives.

Pilot: Scope

The extent and size of the project, campaign or launch will influence the scope of content, deliverables and timeframe. It will also affect the delivery mechanisms you use and whether you need to bring in new technologies, systems or personnel.

Is it full digital implementation or only social media? If it's email marketing, have you segmented your database? Are you targeting prospects only or looking to engage existing customers too?

There are potentially lots of moving parts involved. After all, this is going to be a real execution with real communications being seen by real people.

"Do not let what you can not do interfere with what you can do."
– John Wooden

This is why I believe perfect practice makes perfect. Yes, your pilot is going to be in a semi-controlled environment, but to get the insights you need, you have to put content out in the public domain.

So it's worth investing time in looking at all aspects to ensure you've got everything covered.

Once again, you should consider how you're going to achieve your ultimate goal(s). Then work backwards and map out the activities, touch points, messaging, and any ideas you have that could make your pilot really 'pop.'

As you now know, regularity and consistency of content are important. It's better to post three times per day every day on your Instagram account, rather than uploading 10 photos one day, nothing for three days, and so on.

The wonderful thing about the digital revolution is you can prepare your content in advance. You can plan most of your ideas and the text you want to use ahead of time. It will then be drip fed according to the schedule you've pre-programmed.

A great way to organise your content for this very purpose is by creating a framework or calendar.

Each day of the month your content is mapped out so you'll know exactly what's being published on which day and on which platform.

And then you can have each piece of content posted on your social media platforms automatically.

"The meaning of life is not simply to exist, to survive, but to move ahead, to go up, to achieve, to conquer."
– Arnold Schwarzenegger

Remember, content should be treated like a conversation. It should invite engagement and provide your audience with something interesting or entertaining.

Explore and execute stories that can be fluid – stories that you can use across different channels. Just be mindful of the different nuances of each platform. You shouldn't be just copying and pasting across your digital assets.

Create story narratives that have longevity and can continue over time. This will help your audience understand the context of each story and keep them interested.

Feel free to vary the length and see what your audience responds to. Use a variety of visuals too – images, GIFs and videos can all be used to grab attention and help communicate your message.

And like the most important part of any conversation, it's about listening. So ensure that your content plan includes how and who is responsible for responding, interacting and analysing.

There are plenty of tools, such as Hootsuite or Sprout Social that can help you do this effectively.

Because you're replicating the eventual rollout of your strategy, you must be clear about exactly what you want your audience to do.

You can't predict how people will respond, but it's a useful exercise to try and understand whether you'd like them to engage, comment, learn, share or click.

"The successful warrior is the average man, with laser-like focus."
– Bruce Lee

That way, you can replace, refine or continue with more of the same, depending on your analysis. Once again, what can be measured can be improved.

As well as providing key insights into the viability and scalability of your project(s), a pilot helps you identify potential challenges and new opportunities.

It can also help you understand whether any changes or flexibility are required in approach, scope and direction.

Pilot: Resources

How long should your pilot last for?

Depending on the complexity of your business and its objectives, one-to-three months should be more than enough.

You want to ensure you have enough data to give you the feedback you're looking for. Equally, you also don't want to overcomplicate it.

Make sure you're clear on the role of everyone in your team and whether you need external expertise. If you're using your internal team, do they need training prior to the project?

What about technology, hardware, production (print or digital collaterals)?

Ensure you factor these into to your preparations. They will influence your pilot launch date and whether you need to engage with third party suppliers.

"Pressure is a word that is misused in our vocabulary. When you start thinking of pressure, it's because you've started to think of failure."
– Tommy Lasorda

And think about how you can monitor and deal with potential challenges and bumps in the road during the pilot. Making sure you have over compensated on content is a good start.

From my experience of working with hundreds of SMEs – as well as large corporations – very few actually implement a pilot. I can't emphasise enough how important it is.

It gives you the chance to test drive different strategies and approaches. It enables you to test logistics, communications and team coordination.

It also allows you to identify any potential deficiencies or gaps in training and skills.

Once you've completed your pilot, you'll have a set of results and insights that are like gold dust. But what do you do with them?

"I have always liked a challenge."
– Damon Hill

ASPIRE
Step Four: Investigate

The digital revolution has transformed the way you can market your business. Previously, marketing was (for the most part) expensive and time consuming.

And as a business owner you'd be very limited in what you could do and how many people you could reach.

Even for companies that could afford it, marketing was a bit of a minefield. They would spend enormous amounts and hope their message got in front of as many of their audience as possible.

It was essentially a numbers game, as they adopted more of a scattergun than a strategic approach. Companies were simply throwing their marketing budget at a campaign and using their best guesswork to hit their numbers.

But marketing in a digitally connected world is different. Today, you can plan your strategies using precise data that gives you all the insights you need.

And the results of your pilot programme will help you to do that.

The reason we conduct an audit and then a pilot programme is to assess what's working and what isn't. To understand where improvements can be made and perhaps where none are required.

Everything from your website, customer interactions, feedback, engagement and your processes.

"I'm a person who really doesn't dwell on the past."
– Ronnie Lott

Having been there myself, I know it's tempting to want to skip this step. But it's like a link in a chain – remove it and the whole connection breaks.

To achieve optimal results and understand what's working and what isn't, you must work through this step with as much energy as the other five steps. It's the launch pad for the roll out of your campaigns and strategies.

The data you'll have access to allows you to make immediate improvements by evaluating and measuring real-life numbers whenever you want. You can perform ad-hoc analysis and monitor project and campaign results.

Most importantly, you can make tweaks and enhancements as you go. This allows you to quickly understand the impact of any changes.

The end result is the ability to form predictions about future interactions: what content does your audience enjoy engaging with? What words or phrases do they respond to? What offers do they find most appealing? This is powerful stuff.

It can help elevate your growth potential, enhance execution of ideas and increase leads, conversions and sales. The ability to understand where to deploy your activity and energy to maximise your ROI is why this stage of ASPIRE is so critical.

Let's look at some specific benefits that you can use in your business by investigating and understanding the insights gained from a pilot.

"Everyone has tests in their life. They come in lots of different forms. You want to come out positively at the other end, and that's what I focused on doing."
– Brian O'Driscoll

Personalisation

Content is somewhat of a buzzword these days. Most business owners know it's important, but few are creating, curating or sharing truly engaging content on a daily basis.

As we continue to be bombarded with content on social and traditional media, we're quickly becoming immune. Many people just scroll through their social feeds or email without really taking much (if any) in.

Therefore you must deliver content that stands out and connects with your audience on a different level.

Personalisation is proven to drive results. It can cut through the clutter and help shine a spotlight on your brand.

It can help reduce marketing spend and deliver a significant uplift in engagement and sales. And I'm talking about more than just sending emails or communicating by using the person's name.

In a world of 24/7 connectivity, consumers want content that is informative, relevant and engaging. And if they can't get it from you, they'll turn to another brand that can.

The good news is that data isn't just about the numbers, it can give you a deeper understanding of your audiences' profiles. This knowledge will allow you to create customised messaging, campaigns and even products and services.

You can now deliver the right message or solution, to the right audience, at the right time.

"You can't control what anyone else does, you can only control what you do!"
– Greg Rutherford

Connectivity

Are you succeeding in creating engagement and brand awareness? Are your follower numbers increasing? What are your social media statistics telling you?

Investigate the likes, comments, shares, followers and retweets during the pilot stage. Have you noticed any uplift? Did you meet or exceed your own expectations?

Were you monitoring clicks, conversions and traffic to your website from your social channels? If so, did you notice any distinct patterns, such as the best times to post your social content?

You can do this quickly using any number of tools, or you can check it manually if you prefer.

Another area you can evaluate is whether your audience prefers shorter, punchier messaging or longer, more detailed posts. And what about visuals?

Dig deep into the data to understand whether your audience prefers videos, images, gifs, infographics or slides. It might seem like a little work, but it's well worth it.

Once again, there are tools or specialists that can help you with this.

What these insights give you is the power to leverage your data to provide multi-channel experiences. You can also accelerate the journey to achieving 7/11/4 and the trust that comes with it.

"If you quit every time things don't go your way, then you'll be quitting all through your life."
– Evander Holyfield

By extending your reach across multiple channels, you can take the conversation beyond just social media or email.

Productisation

What if you could create more products and services that you're absolutely certain your audience is interested in? This is where data is once again your friend.

With a little strategic thought, planning and listening, your social media channels can deliver these exact insights from your audience. By actively listening you can also uncover valuable intelligence from online discussions, topical blogs, and keyword-driven trend analysis.

Imagine being able to listen in to unfiltered conversations, getting a clear understanding about their experiences, habits, preferences and challenges. How would this benefit your business and influence your ability to serve your customers with even more value?

Developing a better understanding of your audience is no longer a luxury – it's a strategic necessity. It's also no longer a project that you have to hand over to a market research company.

In the fast-moving digital ecosystem, new platforms, technologies and consumer expectations are changing how they make decisions. This is the single biggest such shift in history.

Consequently, people are now very selective in how they choose the companies that they give their hard-earned cash to.

And there's one generation in particular.

"Virtue lies in the struggle, not in the prize."
– Adam Gilchrist

Millennials make up about a quarter of the UK's population. And as they approach their prime working and spending years, they will soon have a significant impact on the economy.

They have grown up in the midst of the digital revolution and in an age of globalisation and economic disruption.

The effect of this is that they're more tech savvy and turn to their mobile phones for everything they need.

They have become accustomed to ordering food and transport via apps. They research product and service reviews on YouTube.

When it comes to contacting you, they would much rather direct message or 'chat' to your customer service team than actually speak to them.

Consequently, they have different needs and expectations. They are used to convenience, customer-centric experiences and products and services tailored to their specific needs.

And for them, social interaction is important – both with their friends and with brands. They will share their experiences in real time across their social profiles and interact with their friends who are doing the same.

This is why you need to be where they are. Any once you're there, why you need to listen, engage and interact.

"I never left the field saying I could have done more to get ready and that gives me piece of mind."
– Peyton Manning

And this is where – with some thought and creativity – you can tailor what you deliver and give people exactly what they want.

Opportunities

Having completed your pilot, think about what have you've learned from all the key data and what you can do with it.

Are you clear on where to focus more of your efforts and the areas you need to develop further? What about activities that bombed?

And don't worry, it happens to everyone. There is no such thing as failure in business – I prefer to think of it as learning.

Today, consumers are looking for more than just a product or service. They want a relationship with your brand, a sense of community and for you to genuinely care about them.

This is why for you, it *has* to be about more than just the money. Once again, this ties in to your 'why,' your purpose, your mission.

And in the digital revolution, you have the tools you need at your disposal to connect with your audience and create the unique experiences they crave. This is something that just 15 years ago would have been completely out of reach.

But not today.

Through your social media and other digital assets, you can provide enormous value.

"Once something is a passion, the motivation is there."
– Michael Schumacher

With so many content options, you can keep your messages fresh through video, GIFs, infographics and other visuals.

And because data allows you to see what your audience prefers, you can give them more of the same.

Once you get into it, it's easy to get carried away – a bit like a kid at Christmas. But always remain tactical, focus on quality over quantity and don't spam people.

Having a sound strategy in place, as opposed to using random, off-the-cuff tactics, will help you achieve this. Results will come, but they won't happen overnight.

You have to be patient.

Your tactics and strategies will evolve over time, as will your business' journey and indeed, the digital revolution.

But one objective should always remain constant. You must focus on what your audience wants from you before you ever consider focusing on what you want from them.

You must give, give and give again.

For the most part, that will involve producing helpful, engaging, educational, intriguing, entertaining content.

From storytelling and entertainment to free advice and unique insights into you, your business and why you do what you do.

Let your audience get to know you better.

"Life comes down to honesty and doing what's right. That's what's most important."
– Bob Feller

Share your journey with honesty and integrity and watch what happens.

It's no longer about being (just) a gym, tennis academy, online retailer or sports physiotherapist. In the digital revolution, every business must become a media company.

You need to distribute content where your audience is spending the most time – online.

So, having investigated the results of your pilot, you can see the value of implementing a strategy and how it performs under real market conditions.

Of course, this was a **small-scale test-run. But** it should still provide you with enough information so you're able to identify the elements that worked well and correct those that didn't.

This exercise may also throw up some very interesting data. Perhaps it's given you additional insights, allowing you to develop new and exciting products and services for your customers.

In addition, it may have opened your eyes to potential partnership opportunities or even new markets that you hadn't previously considered.

It's now time to go all-in, put your faith in everything you've learned so far and roll out your strategy. The hard (but exciting) work starts now.

"When you are good at something, make that everything."
– Roger Federer

A S P I R̲ E
Step Five: Roll Out

It's the moment of truth.

You've evaluated the data from your pilot. You've refined your strategy and some of your messaging. It's now time to unleash and execute a results-driven strategy.

You may be a little nervous or even apprehensive. But it's important to understand this is a case of the tortoise versus the hare.

Take your time, stick to your strategy and objectives and let the data guide you along the way. It will tell you – as it did during your pilot – what's working and what needs tweaking.

It's always worth doing one last check to ensure you're fully prepared. Does your team understand their role in this strategy? Are any partners clear about the contribution they'll make?

Are all the necessary technologies and systems in place? Is everyone clear on the timelines for this execution?

Communication throughout is vital. Everyone should be on the same page and aware of deadlines, amendments and any additional tasks.

Rather than have everyone in your team emailing or messaging, you could use a project management software.

Now, before you panic at the prospect, let me explain why.

"Struggling and suffering are the essence of a life worth living."
– Dean Karnazes

Firstly, it brings all communications under individual tasks and projects, to avoid miscommunication or confusion. Also, many are easy to use and free.

Our team uses Asana, for example, an amazing free tool that makes it easy to stay on top of each project.

Other options include Basecamp and Trello, but ultimately it's about finding what you're comfortable with and what works best for your team.

Each system allows you to break work into manageable chunks for the team. You can assign project leads, so everyone knows who's responsible.

You're also able to divide tasks into smaller parts, or show additional steps to complete an overall task.

Ensure each task is completed on time by setting a due date and deadline. You can also attach any documents to be shared with others with ease.

In fact in Asana, tasks can be viewed on their own calendar, as well as your work calendar – so it's very flexible.

And everyone receives reminders in their email inbox of any activity, milestones, deadlines, etc. I highly recommend using one – they really do make life easier.

Applying What You've Learned

Having reached this stage in the book, I'm hoping you've learned some critical insights about the digital revolution.

"The more difficult the victory, the greater the happiness in winning."
– Pelé

Why it exists, how it continues to evolve, what the future (potentially) holds and what the risks are for not embracing it and riding the wave.

We've discussed the importance of having a website that delivers ROI for your business. It should clearly differentiate you from your peers, emphasise your credentials, build trust, and generate enquiries and leads.

Most importantly, it should feed in to your strategic objectives.

I've continually emphasised that there's never been a better time to be a business owner. Today, as well as being quicker and more agile than the big boys, small can also give the impression of being big.

You can create more quickly, distribute more quickly, react more quickly. And whilst you can't outspend them, you can outsmart them on a playing field that is now more level than it's ever been before.

Possibly the sternest challenge businesses have right now is the speed at which the digital evolution is taking place.

The delivery of television and radio advertising hasn't changed much in the last 50 years, but the digital world is transforming year on year.

"Most talented players don't always succeed. Some don't even make the team. It's more what's inside."
– Brett Favre

It's a unique era – where brands and consumers have the ability to create and consume content at scale. Just imagine, less than 20 years ago, distributing visual content would have cost hundreds of thousands of pounds.

But the advent of the internet and the smartphone means anyone can create and distribute en masse.

And this is a prime example of the speed of the evolution: the smartphone. A decade ago it didn't even exist, but today there are almost as many smartphones in the world as there are people.

The upshot is you must ensure all of your content can be viewed perfectly on a mobile device, as well as a PC. But as the digital revolution continues to march on, many businesses are still dragging their heels.

This isn't the future, it's today. And those that ignore this fact may not be here tomorrow.

Brands must also realise the major influence in this trend is the role social media plays in many people's lives. In the UK, 78 per cent of over 18s use Facebook regularly, there are around 19 million Instagram accounts and 45 per cent of the population is on Twitter.

No Excuses

There really is no reason for not consistently creating great content around you, your brand and your products or services. And as you've discovered, time is not an excuse. This should be plugged into your weekly schedule. Make it a priority.

"I demand more of myself than anyone else could ever expect."
– Julius Erving

We all admire particular individuals, whether it's Roger Federer, Tom Brady, Lionel Messi, Serena Williams or whoever.

And whilst fans get to see the finished product performing on the world stage, they might not necessarily understand the journey it took to reach such heights.

It's the same for you – commit to a schedule and above all, make a start. Keep videos and blogs relatively short to begin with, if that helps.

But, like riding a bicycle, repetition will give you the necessary experience to get better and feel more comfortable.

When it comes to videos, don't worry (too much) about producing the highest quality in terms of sound and lighting.

Smartphones are the perfect tool to get you started and will deliver a personable style of production that your audience will relate to.

Don't believe me?

Check out some of Gary Vaynerchuk's early stuff. The lighting is less than perfect, some of the audio is echoing and it's not filmed using sophisticated video equipment.

But it's engaging, interesting and stands out.

"Training can be monotonous, and it is hard work, but you never lose sight of why you are doing it. Every single effort of every single session counts in the months and years leading up to a big event."
– Sir Chris Hoy

Having started Wine Library TV in 2006, he grew it from $3 million to $60 million. Vaynerchuk subsequently co-founded VaynerMedia, a digital agency now worth an estimated $150 million. You could say he knows a thing or two about this stuff.

In fact, I recommend you watch plenty of his material. His style is energetic, enriching, enlightening and entertaining – with a few f-bombs thrown in for good measure.

I'm not suggesting you copy him. But he provides such valuable free advice and insights that even if you find his style polarising (which many do), the value he delivers is, in my opinion, unparalleled.

By continuing to learn and apply yourself, you'll become a better storyteller. You'll begin to grasp the nuances of each social media platform.

You'll also get a better understanding of what interests your audience on each platform.

This is an all too often overlooked aspect of communicating in  the digital revolution. It's not about arbitrarily firing off as many messages as you can, just to try and be visible. There has to be an emphasis on quality.

As our attention span continues to shift and diminish, it's become an extremely valuable commodity. Yet many businesses still don't 'get' it.

"If you wait, all that happens is that you get older."
– Mario Andretti

Instead of looking to educate and entertain, they churn out content lacking in both thought and creativity. Much of this content is focused on them and their needs, not their audience.

This is a huge mistake and you'd think they would know better.

But in the digital revolution, the key to being heard is not through self-promotion. You must connect and engage with your audience.

The two-way conversation wins. It's about listening, engaging and offering value for your reader. Focus on publishing content that they can relate to, that they want to consume.

By doing so, you can nurture a relationship that will inspire them to engage with your brand, and who knows... perhaps become a customer.

"My motivation is tomorrow. Just one day at a time."
– Rafael Nadal

A S P I R <u>E</u>
Step Six: Enhance

There's a Japanese philosophy I discovered through Tony Robbins around a decade ago that has stuck with me every since. It focuses on developing continuous improvements, eliminating waste and enhancing efficiency in your business.

This philosophy helped rebuild post-World War II Japanese industry to become what it is today. It's also the foundation of why Toyota is (at the time of writing) the world's largest manufacturer of vehicles.

The name of this philosophy: Kaizen.

Although you're not a multi-billion pound car manufacturer, you can still benefit from the same principles. They'll enable you to identify an opportunity, analyse the process, develop and implement an optimal solution and study the results.

Once you've implemented your strategy, you should look to review and enhance it every month. This is in essence no different to Step Four, where you investigated the activity undertaken in your pilot. However this time, you're going to be doing it on an ongoing basis.

Tracking and measuring are essential to know whether your activity is getting you closer to your goals. What can be measured can be improved. So each month you must track and analyse your data with the aim of optimising your activity.

"Take those chances and you can achieve greatness, whereas if you go conservative, you'll never know. I truly believe what doesn't kill you makes you stronger."
– Danica Patrick

Look for any trends, other meaningful insights and any potential new opportunities. And each month you rinse and repeat. This is how to enhance your performance, productivity and results.

It should be an ongoing process because – as with any business – there will be situations out of your control that you need to adapt to.

But by getting into the habit of manoeuvring when required, you'll be able to quickly respond to challenges that come from leftfield.

This also applies to situations you *are* in control of. Perhaps you want to launch a new product or service, or make changes to your existing offering?

Each scenario will most likely require you to alter your approach, messaging, target audience or all three.

But by conditioning yourself to respond to such circumstances, you'll adopt a solutions-focus mentality. And in turn, you'll feel you can still elevate output, performance and activity, no matter what is thrown at your business.

Here are some top tips for driving continuous improvement across your digital footprint.

Website Enhancements

In the digital world, this is more commonly known as conversion rate optimisation (CRO), but this is merely semantics.

> *"Blood, sweat and respect. First two you give. Last one you earn."*
> – Dwayne Johnson

It's the process of optimising your website to increase the chances of your visitors taking or completing a specific action.

This typically involves elements of copywriting, visual design, psychology, user experience and testing different versions of website content.

Because regardless of how well your site is designed or how many visitors it receives, by making incremental enhancements, your site can always achieve more.

It's also important to understand that results can take a little time, too. There is no silver bullet, despite what you may have seen promoted on the internet.

The process needs time because you'll be testing a number of different elements across your website. This ensures you're basing improvements on real data and not gut feeling or the opinions of others. Real data trumps everything.

And to get a precise understanding of what's working, you should only focus on one element on each page at a time.

If you try and analyse more than one – for example, a video and a certain colour of call-to-action button – you'll never be sure which element helped increase (or decrease) engagement or response rates.

To give you an example of what I mean, let's look at the first of four specific areas you can work on to improve your website's performance.

"If you don't want to be the best, then there's no reason going out and trying to accomplish anything."
– Joe Montana

A/B Testing

In simple terms, A/B testing allows you set up two versions (page A and page B) of the same page and test different elements, such as a video, call to action or order button.

What happens is, as visitors arrive on your page, 50 per cent are presented with page A and 50 per cent with page B.

For example, you might try a green order button on your 'A' page and a red one on your 'B' page, to see which works best.

After a period of time (depending on the number of visitors, this could be a couple of days to one month) you may notice there is a bias one way or the other.

Once you have a 'winner,' you can create another A/B test using another colour versus the winner of your first test. Your aim is now see if you can beat it. And so on.

You may also want to test the text you use for your call to action on the order button. Depending on what you're selling, will "*order now*" outperform "*go to cart*" or would "*learn more*" be better than "*get started?*"

Of course, the type of call to action you use will differ in the case of a free giveaway versus an actual monetary transaction. But the principles are the same.

The button isn't the only element that can be tested. Your videos, images, headlines and on-page copy are all fair game. Any element on any of your pages can be tested. And if testing means a chance of increasing conversion, then why not do it.

"It's not bad to get blocked – it's terrible to stay blocked."
– Ken Norton

Visitor/Customer Journey

Think back to Step One of the ASPIRE process, and the importance of creating a customer avatar. This is another instance of why it's so critical for your business.

Enhancing the user journey on your website is about understanding their point of view. Don't panic, this doesn't mean you need to be a behavioural expert.

But what you are trying to do is put yourself in their shoes and map out what they are potentially likely to do or be looking for when they reach a particular page.

So, based on your customer avatar, you could ask questions like: what motivates or concerns them? What information might they find useful? What are they most likely to click on? What journey could they take through your website before making some type of commitment?

And by commitment, I mean an action like subscribing to your newsletter, requesting information, or clicking the order button.

Thinking about the journey they could take upon reaching your site helps you understand your audience more effectively. It also allows you to provide better experiences, solutions and value where and when they require it.

And whilst you may at first believe this is impossible – think again. Yes, customers and first-time visitors have different needs.

"You should never feel comfortable. There is something wrong if you are. You should always feel under threat, on the edge of your seat and pushing yourself."
– Damon Hill

But this is why you should design specific pages of your website for different types of web visitors and their interests by using tactics such as tailored content and individual offers, promotions, etc.

It's no different to designing displays and staging in a sports apparel retail outlet, for example. In retail, layouts are designed specifically to enhance the experience. Your website should serve exactly the same purpose.

In a store, the window display should be welcoming and entice people in. Once inside, you want to create a great first impression. The layout should lead visitors naturally, without being pushy, so they gain maximum exposure to your products.

Equally, you'll want to create 'breaks' by using displays, 'just arrived' new product lines and other tactics, so they don't just rush through and out of the door.

Of course, you want your staff to be available and helpful, without being overly keen or too salesy. All these elements can create an amazing experience every time people visit you.

And so it is with your website. When you use data, rather than guesswork, you get an accurate and interesting outside-in view of how visitors interact with your site.

By focusing on their desired needs and outcomes, you and your team can maximise the number of holes you plug and create opportunities to increase engagement, interest and eventually conversions.

"Some people want it to happen, some wish it would happen, others make it happen."
– Michael Jordan

Analysing Analytics

Google Analytics might be the most underrated and underused software out there – particularly for business owners. This free software gives you a wealth of useful CRO data, enabling you to track web visitor conversions.

It also provides insight into everything leading up to a conversion and any visitor interactions that *do not* lead to conversions.

I keep talking about conversions, conversions, conversions, right? So what are they? Whilst many people believe they're related to revenue or customer acquisition, in this case they aren't. They are the completion of desired micro-actions within your website.

For example, it could be an action such as requesting more information, subscribing to your newsletter or video series, or downloading a free guide or report.

By thinking about your website visitors' journey and how you believe they interact with your site, you'll uncover a number of valuable questions.

What information would they need as they arrive on your site? What additional resources are they looking for to solve their challenges? Think about how this relates to your site.

The beauty of Google Analytics is that it will help fill in the blanks. As well as tracking exactly how people arrive at your website, you can also see the pages they look at and how much time they spend on them.

"Never set limits, go after your dreams, don't be afraid to push the boundaries."
– Paula Radcliffe

Analytics also gives you tangible data about the search terms your visitors are typing into Google to find you. It also tells you how many pages they look at per visit.

All of this can be used to make improvements to your content, layout, messaging and customer acquisition.

Ask Your Audience

Having an abundance of data to analyse and make adjustments in your business is invaluable. But you would be shocked at just how many businesses are sitting on tonnes of critical insights that never see the light of day.

In addition to the more scientific approach of crunching numbers, you can also go back to basics. Surveying your users is still a popular way of collecting feedback and ideas.

One of the keys to a successful survey is asking the right questions at the right time in the right quantities.

So think about the strategic objectives of your survey and don't ask for too much, too soon or too often.

The types of insights you might be interested in could include:

- How satisfied your customers are
- Why they chose to buy from you rather than your competitors
- What convinced them to cancel their membership or purchase
- What additional (educational) information you could provide them with

"Practice makes permanent."
– Sir Bobby Robson

- Whether they would be interested in the new product or service you're developing
- How did they first hear about you – particularly if they *didn't* find you online

My advice: keep it simple and questions short and crisp. Make sure the survey can be completed in around two minutes, otherwise you run the risk of people losing interest.

As always, it should be written in clear language and represent your brand's voice. It also shouldn't include obviously leading, overly personal or biased questions.

You might also want to offer a small incentive for those that complete the survey.

Enhancing Your Social Media

Social media has featured heavily in this book and for good reason. In the hyper-connected world we live now live in, the number of hours spent posting and sharing content on Facebook, Twitter and Instagram continues to increase exponentially.

In fact, 50 per cent of the time spent on mobile devices is purely on social media. If you hadn't already realised, this explains my constant banging of the social media drum.

Actions that you take in your business should always feed into and contribute to your goals.

"The difference between a successful person and others is not a lack of strength, not a lack of knowledge, but rather a lack of will."
— Vince Lombardi

Therefore your social media goals might include increasing brand awareness, improving engagement, enhancing audience experience or generating more leads.

Once you've defined your overall goals, it's time to get super specific. You've probably heard of the SMART goal framework. It's designed to guide you in setting goals that are **s**pecific, **m**easurable, **a**ttainable, **r**elevant, and **t**imely.

It's important to give them a timeframe so you can break down the activity required to hit your objectives into more manageable chunks.

It also makes the end goals seem less intimidating, allowing you to focus solely on what you need to do each day to work towards achieving them.

And as I mentioned before, concentrating on the activity required to reach your goal, rather the goal itself, is a great way to see and experience progress.

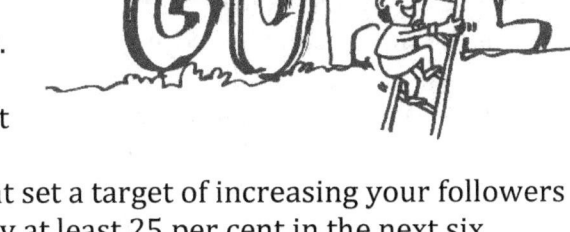

For example, when it comes to brand awareness you might set a target of increasing your followers and/or your reach by at least 25 per cent in the next six months.

So perhaps you focus on posting five times per day, every day, across all your social channels.

"When you fall, get right back up. Just keep going, keep pushing it."
– Lindsey Vonn

It's also wise to focus on engagement, given that (at the time of writing, Facebook and Instagram's) algorithms prioritise posts with higher engagement and make them more visible on people's social media feeds.

Looking to up your lead generation? Why not set an objective of growing traffic to your website by at least 30 per cent in the next three months?

If you have a blog (hint: you should), you may want to drive them there first. By doing so, you're not only furnishing your audience with useful content, you're taking them from social media to your website, but in a nice, subtle way.

It's been an ongoing theme throughout this book, and I'm going to mention it again: consistency. You need to ensure you're producing and sharing a consistent amount of content.

Simply put, the more (good quality content) you put out there the more likely you are to hit your numbers. But the key is to focus on the content – not the numbers. You also want to find that sweet spot between delivering value and commercial messages and/or calls to action.

My preference – and the approach I recommend – is to over-deliver on educational, fun, engaging content and sprinkle in the occasional more sales-oriented communication.

Find Your (Re)Purpose

Here's another great way you can further enhance your social media – *repurposing* your content. But what do I mean by that?

"If nothing else in life, I want to be true to the things I believe in, and quite simply, to what I'm all about."
– Peyton Manning

Repurposing is essentially modifying or breaking your content into smaller chunks to fit a new purpose or platform. For example, a three-minute video could be chunked down into 12 30-second clips.

Although ideally you'd like to do this from the outset, it's more important to get started and commit to producing content day in and day out.

It's a bit like trying to lift weights that are a bit too heavy for you. You could probably do a few reps – even a full set – but you might burn out, get frustrated or injure yourself.

So start slowly and then build up to it.

And once you're comfortable, you can really start to take your content up a notch. Just think about all of your videos, podcasts, interviews, blog posts and articles that could be broken down into micro pieces of content.

For video and audio you may need to hire or use someone you know who has good editing skills. If you have to pay – it'll be worth the investment. Although, you now know the value of partnering and bartering with them – so you can use expertise like this for free with a little creative thinking.

This is working smartly in the true sense of the phrase. It allows you to ensure you have a production line of content that you can use across all your platforms to really up your game.

Like riding a bicycle, you'll find the more content you produce, the easier, quicker and better it will become.

"Life is meant to be a challenge, because challenges are what make you grow."
– Manny Pacquiao

Perfect practice makes perfect. You'll also start to find you become more adventurous in your content – perhaps doing things you never before imagined.

I do hope so. Push yourself out of your comfort zone.

And not all of the content you produce has to be of your own creation. You could also recommend other companies' or individuals' articles and share them with your audience.

If their messages are valuable, your audience will appreciate it – as will those whose articles you've shared. And who knows where that might eventually lead.

Through consistent output, your audience will know to expect your content on a daily basis. Your brand will start to develop a name for itself and your reputation will grow.

As it does, people will start to recognise you and eventually seek you out. You'll also start to attract more and better quality leads and more dream clients.

But as I've mentioned several times, patience and persistence are paramount.

We've almost reached the end of the sixth and final step in the ASPIRE process. But first, let me re-emphasise one of the most important pieces of insight in this book.

As you now know, delivering quality content every day is key in this digital revolution. But if you're marketing to anyone under the age of 45 right now, it's not only key, it's absolutely essential.

"Every strike brings me closer to the next home run."
– Babe Ruth

The mobile device has completely changed the way we live and how we communicate. Smartphones are now so much a part of people's lives that from a marketing standpoint, they've become the new television. In comparison, television is now the new radio.

In the digital revolution, adapting to current trends is vital. Millennials are now spending an average of 18 hours each week consuming content. And over time, this figure is only going to increase.

This means you need to get your brand, messages and content onto social media as often as possible. The more times it's seen on your audiences' feeds, the more chance you have of engaging with them.

When it comes to connecting with millennials, there's plenty of evidence to suggest they prefer storytelling instead of the hard sell. In fact 84 per cent say they don't trust traditional forms of advertising, because it feels inauthentic.

This is no surprise given that most people don't enjoy being sold to. Conversely, many people do enjoy buying.

Sounds counterintuitive, right? But this proves it's all about the approach, engagement and experience you create around your products and services.

This is good news for you for two reasons:

Firstly, this is the way I've recommended you use social media throughout this book. Delivering value, educating, entertaining and being helpful without any expectations in return.

> *"Goals determine what you're going to be."*
> – Julius Erving

If you give more by producing great quality content that really adds value to people's day, you're on the right track. Just think of it from your audience's point of view and create what you believe will interest *them*.

And secondly, most of your competitors aren't doing and may never do this. Instead, they'll continue to pump out a lot of sales-focused, self-promotional messages with no real strategy behind them.

This is the approach to use if you want to kill your engagement potential. It will also ensure your messages lie lost amongst the forest of other *"buy my stuff"* communications.

You don't want to be here. Ever.

"If it doesn't challenge you, it won't change you."
– Fred Devito

PART THREE

WHAT'S NEXT?

So, 12 months down the line and you've successfully applied the ASPIRE process. But what should you do now?

ASPIRE isn't a one-time deal – it's designed to produce ongoing improvements.

You should therefore continue to use the six steps every year to review the health of your marketing, set your new 12-month strategy and ramp up your performance.

But having mastered the fundamentals and with the right framework and firm foundations in place, you're now in a position to really intensify your efforts.

And so in this final chapter, I am going to give you additional, actionable insights you can use that build on everything you've learned so far.

Working in your industry, you'll know more than most that with hard work, dedication and self-belief, tomorrow you can be a little better than you are today. And of course the very same incremental improvements that lead to excellence in the sports and fitness arena, are perfectly aligned to business.

This is where the GROW principle comes in to play. By applying four key growth components, you have the opportunity to add extra impetus to what you've achieved with ASPIRE.

> *"Desire! That's the one secret of every man's career. Not education. Not being born with hidden talents. Desire."*
> – Bobby Unser

I am going to share with you key strategies I've experienced first-hand, have learned and continue to learn. And that last bit is important – *continue to learn* – because I believe you never stop learning.

You can always learn more to give more, contribute more and live more. So, let's get to it.

Open Your Mind To New Possibilities

Life is often a succession of lessons. Once you close your mind to other possibilities, you're closing yourself off to new opportunities that are out there waiting for you.

I developed a whole new perspective on life and business through interactions with my five-year-old daughter, Daisy. Children don't have the preconceptions, conditioning or baggage that many adults accumulate throughout their lives.

In most cases, they aren't afraid to try something new and are unperturbed by making mistakes. They're rarely confined by fears of failure or humiliation. Some of the best lessons we learn are from mistakes and they can sometimes open doors to new and exciting opportunities.

Daisy's favourite question among the many she asks me daily – and one that I never tire of hearing – is *"why?"* She's continuously curious to find out more and to learn, explore and discover.

She's always questioning the status quo. If you have children, I'm sure you can relate to this.

"The problem isn't me thinking I can achieve any goal I set for myself, the problem is you projecting your own self-doubt onto me."
– Ronda Rousey

We can learn so many things from children. But above all, we should always be looking to learn something new each week.

GROW Step One: Generate Partnerships

Partnerships. I briefly touched on them in the strategy step in the last chapter. And I promised you I'd elaborate a bit more on how powerful they can be.

During this chapter, you'll learn how and why you should always be exploring partnership opportunities. I'll also give you some ideas on where to find them.

You can learn and achieve so much by partnering with the right people and businesses. They can help you develop and apply best practices to your ideas.

They can also enable you to deliver more value to more people more quickly. And accessing new partners has never been easier than in the digital revolution.

I use partnerships in two main areas of my business: with suppliers and with what I call 'growth partners.' Let me explain how it works for me.

In my first business, I made a number of mistakes. One in particular was the need to constantly be in control. It was *my* business and I wanted to do it *all*.

So, I spread myself thinly, doing everything from marketing, sales, and networking – to aspects I hated such as admin and basic bookkeeping. I wore many hats in that business.

"To succeed... you need to find something to hold on to, something to motivate you, something to inspire you."
– Tony Dorsett

But success is very rarely achieved in isolation. In sports, whether you're part of a team or you compete individually – there is always a supporting cast of coaches, nutritionists, physiotherapists, psychologists, and more.

It's no different in business. But I learned the hard way. Don't waste your time and energy working on aspects you don't enjoy or where you have no experience. Don't make the same mistakes I did.

Partnering With Suppliers

This requires you to be brutally honest about your own weaknesses, skill gaps and business priorities.

I was guilty of trying to do too many things at once and found it hard to let go. This is often the case when you're extremely passionate about your business.

Working with partners who are experienced in their field will free up more of your time to focus on your core competencies. You'll also be able to spend more time *on* your business, rather than *in* it.

Once you've identified these areas (it could be admin, sales calls, replying to enquiries), approach partners you know and trust or ask for recommendations. Be sure to do your own research for any potential partner you don't know directly.

You need to be sure a partner is the right fit and can deliver what they're promising before you enter into a relationship. This will likely mean you need to meet or video call with them to 'interview' them.

"If you go around being afraid, you're never going to enjoy life. You have only one chance, so you've got to have fun."
– Lindsey Vonn

What is your initial impression of them? Do they share your values? And do they have the type of skillset you're looking for?

Once you've selected a partner, it's important to establish clear objectives. Both parties must be on the same page if you're going to have any chance of success.

Be clear on exactly what you want to get out of the partnership, and understand what your partner wants to achieve too.

You may be thinking you can't afford to bring multiple partners on board. But whether you're bootstrapping it or not, why not work out a way you can barter your services with suppliers. It just requires a little out-of-the-box thinking.

For example, you could offer your accountant a discount to use your facilities or offset the cost of buying your products against the cost their services. Do they have a son, daughter, niece or nephew that's interested in what you offer? Perhaps you can strike a mutual deal?

Be creative and never be afraid to ask – you'll be pleasantly surprised by the results.

And it's always a good idea to do a little research beforehand, to see if there are any obvious opportunities based on their personal or professional interests.

If not, make that part of your discussion when you first speak with them.

"Everything is practice."
– Bill Shankly

I've used this previously with several suppliers and most of the time they don't hesitate in expressing their interest in some kind of deal. Sometimes, once you plant the seed with them, they're the ones that come up with a great barter idea. This really does work.

We recently partnered with a videography company and offered to write their website content in return for a series of 'free' videos and editing. You're only limited by your own imagination and the key is for it to be a win/win for everyone.

Partnering For Growth

When done correctly, partnering for growth can give you a pathway to new customers and markets that may not otherwise be available or easily accessible.

It also enables you to deliver products and services through a third party that ideally complements what you're already providing. By finding the right partner(s), you can leverage on their capacity and expertise, whilst giving both sets of customers (yours and theirs) even more added value.

Ask yourself some probing questions: are you struggling to reach or penetrate a particular target audience? Do you have challenges with additional capacity or inventory?

Are any aspects of your products and services seasonal? Would you like to deliver more products and services to your customers?

I'm sure you can think of ones appropriate to your niche and current situation. Brainstorm, get them down and see what ideas you come up with.

"I believe there is room for improvement in every sportsman."
– Lionel Messi

Once again, the key is to be honest with where you are now and ask yourself questions that can help realise your ambitions.

A good place to start is by thinking about businesses that already serve customers and markets you could also serve.

You should also consider products and services that you don't currently offer, but would like to, as they would also benefit your customers.

Due diligence is once again important. Be sure to do your homework before picking up the phone or writing to discuss or pitch your proposal.

A little research and preparation will serve you well and also demonstrate you know what you're doing.

This will also instil confidence in your potential partner – which is exactly the type of first impression you want to create.

When it comes to the groundwork, what should you consider?

Firstly, you need to work out exactly what you are offering a partner. What's in it for them? This isn't just about thinking of yourself.

You need to be sure a partner is the right fit for you and your brand. What can they bring to the party? What is the potential for a long-term partnership?

"I always try to start out with some type of goal. Then I work backward and think of what I need to do to get there, and give myself smaller goals that are more immediate."
– Kristi Yamaguchi

Think about anyone in your mobile phone, network group or LinkedIn contacts. Are they a potential partner? Or might they know someone who is?

Once you've developed a list (the bigger the better), your next step is to refine it into realistic, potential partners. A great place to kick off is by identifying and defining the criteria you're looking for in a partnership.

There are three things I look for to assess compatibility that may help you:

Values And Beliefs

This is number one on my list because for me, it's the most important. You may find a partner that ticks many of the right boxes, but if they don't tick this one, it's a deal-breaker.

I genuinely believe you can't fake it when it comes to a successful partnership. You should be aligned to a shared vision and agree with their core beliefs, values and goals. If it's incongruent, it's probably better to take a pass.

Don't forget, this partnership may impact your reputation one way or another. You don't need to choose the first company that *sort of* feels right. Take your time to decide and choose wisely. And don't be tempted to chase the money.

Complementary Products And Services

The whole purpose of collaborating is to ensure customers – whether they're yours or your partners – have access to a wider choice of products or services.

"If you fail to prepare, you're prepared to fail."
– Mark Spitz

What this *is not*, is about exploiting someone else's skills or database for your own gains. It's about working together to deliver exponential value for both sets of customers.

Therefore, when choosing a potential partner, think about what your clients may benefit from or may have asked about in the past. Did they post on social media asking if you sell or know someone that sells X, Y or Z?

Think about what products and services are a great fit for your customers. Also, see where you can add value to a non-competing business by helping *their* customers, and vice versa. The more you brainstorm, the more ideas will come to you.

Setting Expectations

Once you've established that you're a good fit, it's a good idea to agree on clear objectives and expectations. This helps avoid any unpleasant surprises further down the line.

It's also why step one is so important, because your expectations will likely be linked to the values and vision you have about what you want to achieve and why. It should *always* be about more than the money.

Just as you would with your internal team, set goals and agree on accountability so your partner has absolute clarity on their responsibilities and targets. I believe in approaching all negotiations in a transparent and professional way.

Not just because it's the right thing to do – but it sets the tone for potential future collaborations with the same partner.

"Somebody may beat me, but they are going to have to bleed to do it."
– Steve Prefontaine

A partnership is a two-way street, of course. If you're expecting accountability, you should also give it.

So if part of the agreement involves some work on their part, be sure to reciprocate, even if it might not be necessary.

This is why being selective is critical to the process. You need to be comfortable with any partner you work with, and vice versa.

By working together, you're both serving as extensions of each other's brands – so choose wisely.

What you're looking for is a perfect three out of three for the points above. If it's quite obvious – or you have a gut feeling – that they don't tick at least one box, move on to the next one on your list.

Once you've selected a suitable partner, you should formalise the partnership with some kind of written agreement. You may want to draw up a contract or keep it to a fairly simple email. Either way, you should create something.

This will ensure both parties are clear on their roles and responsibilities and what the potential rewards are.

It's also a nice way to show that you're serious, committed and genuinely value their expertise and input.

"Believe me, the reward is not so great without the struggle."
– Wilma Rudolph

Once everything is signed and sealed, you should revisit the ASPIRE model. Go through each step, just as you would for any other campaign, project or launch. This is where you can add enormous value to the relationship.

Imagine what your partner will think when you plug some or all activity into a robust, proven framework. It will not only demonstrate you're organised and professional, but also that you're a partner with serious upside to offer them.

GROW Step Two: Redesign Your Offering

A big mistake many businesses make – often without even realising – is focusing on only one product or service. Most personal trainers provide personal training. Rugby and football academies provide coaching, for example.

But *why* is this a mistake?

This is another great concept I learned from entrepreneur Daniel Priestley, and I'd like to share it with you because it genuinely is a game changer. It's not about having just one product or service – or even a range of them (although that *is* better) – you need to create an *ecosystem*.

In an ecosystem, each product or service has specific objectives, outcomes and strategically links to the next. It primes your prospects into engaging with you, buying from you and delivers remarkable long-term value.

The different products and services form a logical sequence and also escalate in price. I'll discuss the importance of getting this right and why it's important in a moment.

"Procrastination is one of the most common and deadliest of diseases and its toll on success and happiness is heavy."
– Wayne Gretzky

But here's the secret sauce: the overall aim of this exercise is to create assets that can deliver, whether you are there or not.

Why is this important?

Well, if the majority of your revenue is a result of you being paid for your time, you have a problem. There is only one of you and you can only be in one place at a time. Your business and earning potential will be limited and you'll always feel time poor or overstretched.

So the idea is to package up your offering. Even if you provide services, they can be productised – removing the restriction of exchanging money for time.

What you're doing is repackaging your services into easy to access products that deliver your ideas, insights and expertise.

The end result may be that you only directly contribute 20 per cent of your time to your new suite of products. It may be that 30 per cent is handled by your team or an external partner and 50 per cent delivered through digital assets.

This is where digital products and partnerships come in to their own. You're leveraging technology and other people's time, instead of having to dedicate yourself to every client interaction. This is how you scale a business and remove yourself from doing all of the functional (time consuming) work.

Another advantage of digital products is they can be downloaded, watched, listened to or read at any time of day or night, anywhere in the world.

"If you dream and you allow yourself to dream you can do anything."
– Clara Hughes

It allows you to more quickly create rapport between you and your prospect, while they spend more time 'with' you.

By doing so, you're building the foundations to achieving 7/11/4. It's the start of them knowing, liking and trusting you.

Although this may sound complex or completely different to how you currently operate, it's actually much easier than you think.

And it also complements the ASPIRE methodology perfectly, so you won't have to rethink your strategy.

So let me illustrate this in greater detail by looking at how Apple has created and uses their product ecosystem. Whilst I know they're a multi-billion dollar corporation, they're the perfect model of how and why a product ecosystem works.

And for extra clarity, I'll also give examples from your industry, which should help you starting to think about how this can apply to *your* business.

There are four components to a product ecosystem. They are:

Gifts

Gifts are products or services that should be given free of charge to your prospects, without any commitment. You must therefore ensure you have the capacity and financial capability to deliver them for free.

"There are only two options regarding commitment. You're either IN or you're OUT. There is no such thing as life in-between."
– Pat Riley

They often have a high-perceived value, whilst the cost to you is minimal. This allows you to give them away freely without your accountant losing his hair and your business going bankrupt.

Gifts are designed to provide your prospects with something extremely useful, whilst subtly serving as a lead generation tool.

However, there should be no obvious expectation on your part of receiving anything in return.

This means not asking for email addresses (yet), no follow up sales calls, and no bad feelings if they don't become a customer. At this stage it's all about giving.

This may sound counterintuitive, but it works.

So, let's take a look at how Apple approaches this. Among their gifts are their iTunes app and iBooks. Both are free to download and give you the opportunity to store a selection of free music and books.

These gifts get you acquainted with the brand at no cost. And they're the first rungs on the ladder for potentially becoming an Apple customer.

And what about your business? Do you have a short video series you can give away or some type of educational booklet?

How about a free trial or one hour's consultation? What could be *your* gift to your prospects?

"You can learn a line from a win and a book from a defeat."
– Paul Brown

Products For Prospects

A product for prospects is a low priced offering that allows you to begin a sales conversation with your prospects. Think of it as a bit of a sales icebreaker – a low barrier to entry to starting a serious relationship with your brand.

It should deliver some kind of positive experience or result, further enhancing the bond of trust between you. Ultimately, this product should be working to lead customers towards investing in your main, core product. More about that soon.

Your product for prospects shouldn't compete with your other products, but complement them. And once again, it shouldn't be followed by a barrage of emails, calls or messages to try and upsell your client.

Let them try and see the benefits of the product first.

Apple's products for prospects are their iPod or Apple TV. Although buying either is a relatively small investment, it demonstrates commitment from the customer.

It also shows there is an element of trust in place, which as a business gives you a great foundation to build on.

What can you use to kick start your customer's journey? If you offer a monthly membership, can you offer a one-week package specifically for this purpose?

Do you have a comprehensive video series, set of e-books or a bundle of small products you can package together?

"Success is no accident. It is hard work, perseverance, learning, studying, sacrifice and most of all, love of what you are doing or learning to do"
– Pelé

Your aim at this early stage is to maintain the wow factor and confidence from the gift they received from you.

And by continuing to deliver immense value, the next step for them should be to invest in the third product – your core product.

Core Product Range

These are your main products or services and should offer a complete and transformational solution to the challenges faced by your customers. At this stage, price doesn't and shouldn't come in to play, such is the trust and credibility you've built.

While you can afford to lose a little on your gifts and just about break even on your product for prospects, your core products are different. They should ensure you're paid for the value you deliver, have high margins and build profit for your business.

You want your core products to be among the best in your market and for your customers to become raving fans. Based on the value offered so far and your customers' experiences, they may see you as the only company of your kind that they want to do business with.

And here's another key insight for you – when developing your core products or services, try and provide a range of options. For example, my digital communications agency has Bronze, Silver and Gold packages – all for different levels of challenges and positioned at different price points.

"Things turn out best for the people who make the best of the way things turn out."
– John Wooden

Two of Apple's most popular core products are of course the iPhone and Mac range. If you're a Karate school or sports academy, could you deliver a bundle offer of one month's coaching, video series, educational material and nutrition products?

No matter what niche you're in, you can package products and services together.

By doing so, you can provide higher value, higher ticket options that make you stand out from your competitors and grow your bottom line.

Logical Next Step

The fourth and final component in your product ecosystem is the logical next step. This should only be made available to those that bought one of your core products –and having experienced incredible results, they're now looking for more.

From your perspective, it should add significant profit to your bottom line. This is due largely to the fact that your customer acquisition cost has already been absorbed.

Once again, the logical next step should command a premium price. Having already bought your core product, your client is now looking for more value and solutions.

And it's by delivering this additional product that you really start to see growth and scalability in your business.

What logical next steps does Apple present their customers with?

"A strong mind is one of the key components that separates the great from the good."
– Gary Player

Well, having purchased an iPhone or Mac, you can choose from a wide range of useful services such as iCloud storage, an Apple Music subscription or one-stop service and support for their phone with AppleCare.

As with your core and product for prospects, the key is to ensure your logical next step complements your existing range whilst offering something a little different.

For example, if you sell sports equipment, is there an opportunity to offer coaching, too? Or if you have a tennis school, how about designing specific fitness programmes for your members?

This brings us back to value of partnerships. Having the right collaboration can have a huge impact – you just need to think about what can enhance your existing service.

GROW Step Three: *On* Your Business, Not *In* It

If there's one area that business owners and entrepreneurs often struggle with the most, it's focusing too much on activities *in* their business, rather than *on* it. But why do so many get bogged down by trying to micromanage everything?

In many cases, it's because they believe they can do things better and more efficiently than anyone else. And whilst that might be true, failing to delegate or outsource certain tasks could lead you to suffer burn out, or worse.

Time spent on jobs that others could be doing is time that could be better served on the bigger picture. After all, you're the leader, even if you're a one-man band.

"When people throw stones at you, you turn them into milestones."
– Sachin Tendulkar

I know there are clients that need attention, staff that need managing and tasks that only the CEO can attend to. I know the devil is in the detail and that completing many little tasks *can* make a big difference.

But failing to focus on strategic activities that help drive your business forward is a sure fire way to failure. And I should know.

Rather than trying to do everything, you must be the leader, visionary and troubleshooter.

Set strategic objectives, spot opportunities and focus on growing the business.

And when it comes to the more day-to-day output, empower others. By delegating tasks, your internal and external teams will appreciate the trust and responsibility you're giving them.

Across your business and throughout the six ASPIRE steps, you must identify the core activities you need to apply as the leader of the business.

It's then absolutely critical you develop a system or a culture within your company that maximises your productivity and negates unnecessary interruptions.

I like to approach my days with an outcome focus. I look at what I want to achieve each week and break it down into the most important daily tasks.

"I'm trying to do the best I can. I'm not concerned with tomorrow, but with what goes on today."
– Mark Spitz

This is a system that keeps me organised on a daily basis, so that I know what I'm doing at what time, where, and how it fits in to my business. But the key is to be disciplined and not get distracted.

And I'll be honest with you, to begin with it's not always easy.

You must maintain your schedule as much as possible and emphasise to others that unless it's an absolute emergency, you are not to be disturbed.

This takes some mastering, as in my experience it's a very different approach to how most business owners operate. I even factor in specific times to check my emails, rather than rushing to check my inbox as soon as I hear a notification.

Constantly reading emails the minute you receive them is not an effective use of your time. The same can be said for social media and other 'push' notifications.

This is no different to inviting anyone and everyone to disturb you whenever it's convenient *for them.*

It's not a case of being anti-social or unapproachable. You should encourage your staff to come to you with anything they can't handle, but on *your* terms. Arrange a time each day, 4pm – 5pm for example, when staff can come to you with questions or ideas.

Of course there are always exceptions to the rule, such as time or business critical tasks that absolutely require your input.

"Success is not forever and failure isn't fatal."
– Don Shula

But having as much structure to your day as possible will enable you to stay on track with your workload. You'll also notice your productivity soar.

Personal Brand vs Business Brand

Brand. It's a word we hear all the time. Earlier we discussed exactly what a brand is and why it's important for your business.

But there's another brand you need to consider, create and continually work on. Your own.

As the face of your business, your personal brand is potentially just as valuable as your business brand. It can get your name recognised. It can also create greater credibility, trust and attract more and better quality business.

Your brand should be constantly evolving and growing, along with your business. However, you may decide that your personal brand *is* your business brand, and that you don't need both. And that's fine as it's different for everyone.

Whilst there are arguments for and against having one or the other, I prefer both.

Here's why:

People often connect with real people much easier than they do a brand (more about this later). Personal brands lend themselves more naturally to rapport and relationship building.

"All your dreams can come true, trust me – just work hard and train harder."
– Sir Mo Farah

By telling stories, sharing what you've learned or describing your experiences and struggles, you're being authentic. People will enjoy hearing about your journey, your story. They'll relate, respect and respond to it.

Amazing things can happen when you decide to share your stories and passion with the world. Your personal brand can take on a life of its own, and develop in a natural, organic way.

You start attracting those who share your values and beliefs – those who appreciate the realness and authenticity of your communications. This can have a substantial impact in separating you from your competitors.

There really is no need to 'fake it til you make it,' either. Authenticity wins every time. Hands down.

In the digital revolution, everyone has the opportunity to make their voice heard and build a like-minded following on any platform they choose. This is without question, the most exciting time to own a business.

But while it's never been easier to share your messages with the world, it's also never been more difficult to make yourself heard — or to get people to care. And by care, I mean to really resonate and engage with your message or cause.

Which is why authenticity, transparency, sharing your journey and being relatable is crucial. So, will you sit behind the curtain and hide, or step onto the stage and be heard?

Start thinking about the online assets you already have that you can use to kick-start your brand story. Do you have any videos from your early days? Any photos?

"I try not to worry about things I can't control."
– Paula Radcliffe

If you didn't write about your experiences at the time, I'm sure you could recall key moments during your journey and use them today. Get them down on paper.

You may already have a following, a reputation and an online presence. In which case, how can you leverage and grow that following?

Developing Your Personal Brand

In a 24/7-connected world, every photo you share, every tweet you send and every Instagram story you publish contributes to your personal brand. As you've learned, one of the critical elements of executing a solid communications strategy is to actually have one in the first place.

Many of your competitors won't have one or at best it'll be rather loosely put together. It's the perfect time for you to strike.

As you've heard many times in this book, consistency is the key. In many ways it's better to be the tortoise, rather than the hare. It's about an accumulation of multiple, daily actions.

Every aspect of your communications should be strategic (even the ad-hoc ones) and developing your personal brand is no exception.

But because it has to be strategic, doesn't mean it should be totally scripted. As already mentioned, to succeed in this game, your brand should be a direct reflection of who you really are.

"When you've got something to prove, there's nothing greater than a challenge."
– Terry Bradshaw

This might mean that in videos you swear a bit. Perhaps when writing, your grammar might make your English teacher cringe a little.

It doesn't matter – it's all about ensuring your authentic self shines through in everything you do.

Imagine the amount of work required to build a fake personal brand. Everything would need to be highly scripted. You'd have to keep the act up 24/7 to appear consistent.

You may be raising your eyebrows right now, but I can tell you, there are plenty out there doing just that.

People connect with other people. If you were found out to be faking it, you'd lose any credibility and trust you'd built with your audience. And even if you manage to succeed for a while, you'll always be fearful that one slip up could bring everything crashing down.

And of course, it's also just plain unethical.

Be you, be personable and above all else, be honest. And don't be fearful of talking about your struggles, as well as your successes. The more transparent you are the more respect you will earn.

A Lethal Combination

When used in conjunction with your business brand, your personal brand has the opportunity to exponentially grow your reach.

"I was not the fastest or biggest player but I was determined to be the best football player I could be on the football field and I think I was able to accomplish that through hard work."
– Jerry Rice

Every video you post, every article you publish and every social media post you make has the potential to connect you with more people. Makes sense right?

Think Steve Jobs and Apple – where two strong brands aligned to the same cause was far more powerful than just one. Don't get me wrong, this meteoric rise won't happen overnight, but it will never happen if you don't make a start.

If you're unsure of this personal brand stuff, you're just starting out or you have no real digital presence at the moment, don't panic.

The strength of your brand isn't necessarily the number of followers you have, but the sum of all your online activities.

Following the ASPIRE methodology will help create the right framework for you to go out and do your thing.

Yes, the digital landscape is undeniably noisy, but meaningful content and actions can help you successfully cut through the clutter.

And it doesn't even need to be strategic content that you've necessarily created. It can be your interactions on social media, articles or interviews that feature your thoughts and comments, or case studies and testimonials about your business.

You just have to get started. I know you'll have a mountain of knowledge and insights inside your head and possibly on your PC, phone or hard drive. You just need to get them out in a format that people can consume and act upon.

"I'm motivated by the fear of being average."
– Bryce Harper

GROW Step Four: Winning Through Influence

There are several (many would say annoying) business buzzwords for reaching this stage.

But whatever your definition, from thought leader to influencer and authority to maven, peel away the jargon and it reveals the credibility of being considered a key person in your industry.

There's a specific reason why this is the fourth and final component in the GROW process, and this analogy explains why: you can't develop your muscles without lifting weights. So what exactly do I mean by that?

Becoming well known and respected in your industry is achieved by building a successful business and having a bulletproof brand. It's also about having lots of published content across many touch points and publications.

You have to put the work in first.

Reach this level, and you can more easily cut through the noise and garner attention as someone worth listening to.

The more you immerse yourself in working on your business, the more this will amplify. You'll better understand your audience's problems and freely offer answers to help solve them.

The content you'll deliver will not only be enjoyable, educational and engaging, it will inspire action.

"We don't do things we aren't good at by nature. I wouldn't play basketball because I'm only 5' 1". Find what you enjoy."
– Danica Patrick

You already know your industry well, will have a certain presence (that shouldn't be underestimated) and a variety of connections. I'm sure you also have or can access a great deal of insight on the trends, challenges and talking points in your industry.

To be considered a thought leader in your industry, you should be able to clearly understand the challenges that impact your audience and articulate valuable advice.

It's not about delivering thinly veiled sales pitches to promote your business.

You also need to be patient. What you're producing (from a marketing perspective) is more of a slow burn in terms of return on investment. But new doors will open that you never imagined possible.

Demand for your products and services will increase and you'll effortlessly build new relationships and partnerships. Bigger and better opportunities will fall at your feet, not only in terms of clients but also collaborations.

Your standing in the industry will continue to rise and others will seek you out for advice and opinions. You'll be known as a go-to personality in your sector.

Content + Context

You may have heard the expression 'content is king,' in which case context is queen. This may sound somewhat cryptic or clichéd but it's something the ASPIRE steps are designed to simplify.

> *"If you aren't going all the way, why go at all?"*
> – Joe Namath

Context is the framework and structure you have for creating and publishing your content. This could be the team around you, systems you have in place and the platforms you're using.

By using ASPIRE, you'll set strategic objectives and activities that drive consistent productivity. And by planning ahead of time, you'll know what you're doing on a daily basis, giving you the ability to delegate and outsource more effectively.

By freeing up more of your time, you'll be able to concentrate on bigger things and on moving your business forward. You'll also be able to take more holidays, spend time with those that matter most or just take time out.

These are often 'luxuries' that business owners don't feel they can have.

The emphasis on content is why I talk about the need for every business to be a media business. Get in the habit of consistently producing high quality content. It takes a little sweat equity in the beginning but the payoff can be huge.

As you read in Part One, social media is a great place to start. It gives you an opportunity to deliver sound bites of content to a wide audience and understand what's happening in your industry.

Having got your feet wet by doing this, you may want to start writing a blog. And don't worry, you don't need to be a top-notch writer – simply start by getting your ideas down and then elaborating on them.

"Every day is a new opportunity. You can build on yesterday's success or put its failures behind and start over again."
– Bob Feller

One of the best pieces of advice I was given is to write as you speak – even if your grammar isn't perfect. This will ensure your writing comes across as naturally as possible and has your personality embedded into it.

If you're particularly averse to writing, then why not get audio transcribed? There are plenty of apps and services out there, Rev being just one example, that can do this quite inexpensively.

You simply talk, send the audio off to be transcribed, and voilà!

Your blog is the ideal place to write and share content about industry news, events and trends. It instils and builds confidence in your readers that you know what you're talking about.

It allows you to express yourself and highlight your credentials.

Once it's brimming with useful content, your blog will demonstrate that your business is built upon the solid foundations of your expertise.

And it will increase your digital footprint considerably, so that more people will find you more often by googling topics you've written about.

Focus on the questions your target audience have and provide them with relevant and informative answers.

"If you don't have to drag yourself off the field exhausted after 90 minutes, you can't claim to have done your best."
– Bill Nicholson

Identifying their problems and offering solutions isn't just fundamental to your business success, it's an excellent way to enhance your visibility and notoriety in your industry.

With your blog firmly established, you can further amplify your messages and help others by guest blogging for other popular industry blogs and writing articles in different publications. Be sure to do your research in advance, identify which ones are a great fit and approach them accordingly.

Be persistent. You may need to contact five to get one to say "*yes*," but the rewards are worth the effort.

Public Speaking

These two words can strike fear into even the bravest or most confident person.

But as a leader in your industry, speaking engagements and interviews will present themselves, so why not go where the fear is and bite the bullet.

There are many books that specialise on this topic but I recommend you read *The Book on Public Speaking* by Topher Morrison. It's one of the most comprehensive and easy-to-read books out there.

As with public speaking, so it is with any business tactics. You should start small to begin with.

Perhaps you could get some confidence under your belt by talking at schools, leisure centres or networking events.

"Anyone can achieve great things in their lives if they are willing to work hard, make sacrifices and dedicate themselves to the dream they have."
– Sir Chris Hoy

By this stage, with all the videos you've published, you'll have spoken in front of a camera on many, many occasions. So the concept won't be entirely alien to you.

You're used to sharing insights and new ideas to audiences that you can't see. Now it's time to do it in front of those you can.

I realise this is face-to-face and it's live. You will be nervous (everyone is), you will make mistakes (everyone does), and you will walk away thinking to yourself *"why did I say that?"*

But just like when you were learning to ride a bicycle as a kid – you wobble, lose your balance and fall off – but you get straight back on again. This is all part of the learning process.

Your first five talks won't be as good as your tenth. And once you get to 20 or more, you'll be well on your way.

With some smaller speaking engagements under your belt, you may want to up the ante and speak at industry or specific events. It's always a good idea to do your homework. Perhaps make sure you attend the events you're interested in as a delegate first of all, or see if you can watch the previous edition of the event online.

Do you know any of the people speaking at a particular event? Perhaps you know the organisers? If you have a connection or can be introduced by someone, use it to your advantage. If not, drop them an email with a link to some of your best material. Show them how you can add value to their event.

"If your dream ain't bigger than you, there's a problem with your dream."
– Deion Sanders

Public speaking enables you to create more valuable intellectual property that can be used beyond the roomful of attendees. Ensure you record it (or have access to the recording) so you can repurpose and use it on social media, your YouTube channel and elsewhere.

If the content was valuable for the event's audience, it'll be valuable to other people, too.

Three Benefits Of Having More Influence

Whilst the concept of being a person of influence is certainly not new, it has taken on a life of its own in the digital revolution. Given the ease at which ideas can be created and shared, there's never been a more prolific time in history for thought leadership.

Equally, given the availability of information online and that not everything on the internet should be believed, you need to have the correct positioning in place. This is once again where applying the six ASPIRE steps comes in.

Once you establish yourself as a key person in your industry, prospects and customers will listen to you more. Your peers will sit up, pay attention and respect you more.

And the media, bloggers and other influencers will respond to you more.

By being seen as a knowledgeable resource through your content, you become part of the conversation early in the buying journey. This enables you to answer many questions in advance, overcome potential objections and allow your audience to get to know you.

"The more you seek the uncomfortable the more you will become comfortable."
– Conor McGregor

And of course, this is exactly what you want. To create a relationship, use the 7/11/4 concept and eliminate objections before they have the chance to interfere with discussions further down the line.

This also helps you maintain your premium pricing, as your prospects already understand the value you bring to the table.

There are undoubtedly more than three advantages to having more influence. And whilst digging deeper into more of them should probably be left for another book, I'd like to highlight three that I feel you can easily relate to at this early stage in your journey.

Differentiation

With competition fierce and customers often difficult to come by, being recognised allows you to differentiate yourself in a crowded market.

It can help create a higher demand for your business and alleviate the need to chase leads in an attempt to convert them into sales. Being among the few rather than the many can help attract some of the most valuable clients in the market.

In time, people may associate your brand with well-known, critical thinking, industry-leading ideas and as a highly respected knowledge base. Your employees and partners will see you as a rewarding company to work with.

"An athlete gains so much knowledge by just participating in a sport. Focus, discipline, hard work, goal setting and of course, the thrill of finally achieving your goals. These are all lessons in life."
– Kristi Yamaguchi

Other talented experts may also gravitate towards you, based on your presence in the industry.

Greater Voice

What impact could it have on your business if you were sought out to comment on the key challenges and topics in your sector?

You may be asked to guest blog on a well know influencer's site or be interviewed on local or national radio. What if you were invited onto an industry leading podcast or appeared on TV to answer key questions affecting your customers?

Regardless of the medium, platform or opportunity, this is exactly what you've been working up to all this time. All the hard work, the blood, sweat and tears. This is now your time to shine.

By being among the elite in your industry, opportunities will start stacking themselves – so much so you'll be able to pick and choose the ones you want. May be you're presented with one which isn't a 100 per cent fit, perhaps one comes your way and you're too busy. It's nice to be in a position to be selective.

Ambassador

One of my ambitions when I first set out on my entrepreneurial journey was making a difference outside of my clients. My digital communications agency already supports a couple of charities that are important to our core team.

"You have to free your mind to do things you wouldn't think of doing. Don't ever say no."
– Carl Lewis

But I don't want to stop there, because I know there is so much more I can do.

You may choose to use your industry influence to play a more active role with organisations that are important to you or your family. Think about some of the causes worldwide or closer to home that you're passionate about helping and get in touch with them.

It may be supporting a particular charity, building an orphanage or school, or something else. How might having a bigger platform and a greater profile help you to really make a difference?

Take a friend of mine, fellow entrepreneur Simon Jordan. You can find him on Twitter: @TheSimonJordan and on Instagram: @5ThingsClear.

One morning in June 2017, he was walking on his local beach with his two dogs, as he does most days. But minutes later, he was holding a dying seabird in his hands. A plastic ring was trapped around its head and had been stopping the Manx shearwater – a member of the puffin family – from feeding.

What a truly awful way for this living creature to go and so very avoidable.

Following this harrowing experience, Simon felt he had to take action, and so #5ThingsClear was born. His idea is to inspire people to pickup just five pieces of litter a day, helping to make a positive impact on the environment.

"For sportsmen or women who want to be champions, the mind can be as important, if not more important, than any other part of the body."
– Gary Neville

In just two months the initiative had become a global phenomenon, with many people around the world – including Hollywood actress Pamela Anderson – posting about it on Instagram.

Every day more continue to join in to spread the word in an effort to help save our planet.

I encourage you to find out more about Simon's mission at www.5ThingsClear.com, by connecting with him on social media or by searching for #5ThingsClear on Instagram.

And do get involved. It's a wonderful way to teach children about litter, it's an excellent excuse to get out into the great outdoors – and every little bit helps our planet.

What are you passionate about outside of sports and fitness? What local, national or even international causes have you been thinking about helping, but never got around to – or felt you didn't have the time, money or resources?

As one of the most famous sports brands on the planet so eloquently puts it: "Just Do It!"

"Self-belief is probably the most crucial factor in sporting success. It is the iron in the mind, not the supplements, that wins medals."
– Sir Steve Redgrave

PART FOUR

EPILOGUE

This final chapter is brief, but nevertheless just as important as its predecessors. It also applies, whether you are just starting out on your entrepreneurial journey or have been around the block a few times.

Regardless of how well you know your industry or your area of expertise, things are changing at an alarming rate. Transformation is occurring faster than ever before.

And there are consequences for not staying up-to-date with the latest trends and changes – both in your industry and the digital revolution.

Always Be Learning

I believe every interaction you have on a daily basis, from a chat with a supplier, meeting with a staff member or reading a blog, is a chance to learn something new.

In fact, I make it a prescheduled part of my day to listen to a podcast I've subscribed to, watch a Ted Talk or YouTube channel, or read a blog.

It might be five minutes, 25 minutes or more. But I rarely fail to pick up a least one nugget – and sometimes about subjects I thought I had no interest in. If you keep an open mind, there is always something valuable to learn.

"Whatever you do in your life, always go the distance."
– Ken Norton

It doesn't have to necessarily be new skills – it may just be expanding your knowledge or perspective on a topic.

But I learned around a decade ago that if you're not growing, you're stagnating. And as a person – let alone a business owner – that's the last thing you want.

It's also one of the reasons I invest in business coaches. It's not as some type of status symbol, but rather to learn from those who have been there before you.

They know the pitfalls to look out for and will often share mistakes *they* made, so you won't make the same.

Having a coach, mentor or advisor helps keep you on track, focused and perhaps most important of all, accountable.

Additionally, they'll always provide brutally honest yet constructive feedback, rather than downplaying any errors you've made or weaknesses they see in you.

Odds are you already know how important it is to stay on top of your game. But a friendly reminder never hurt anyone.

You'll also know that when you run your own company, it's sometimes difficult to share your true concerns with people.

If you have a partner, you may not want to bring your problems home with you.

Depending on the type or severity of challenge, it may not be appropriate to discuss it with members of your team.

"Setting a goal is not the main thing. It is deciding how you will go about achieving it and staying with that plan."
– Tom Landry

But having an impartial set of eyes and ears can serve as a confidential sounding board to listen and help provide solutions and ideas to the challenges you're facing.

In closing, let me leave you with three different types of learning that you can acquire, either proactively or reactively.

Livelihood Learning

This applies to industry learning – acquiring knowledge that ensures you're keeping up with trends, aware of what's coming next and so on. You might do this via social media, meeting your peers or attending events.

It's not about broadening your skill set, but keeping up to date with what's going on. It's keeping your finger on the pulse, making sure you aren't missing anything. Staying current.

Think of it like a light physical workout. It will keep your fitness tuned at a particular level so you stay in shape, rather than enhancing your strength or endurance.

Expansion Learning

Expansion learning is about adding knowledge and skills to your armoury that you didn't have before. This could be learning that helps expand your mind, skills or business.

It may be that you subscribe to podcasts, read blogs or books, or watch videos to do this.

Perhaps you are a member of a specialist service, specifically designed to enhance a particular skill. You may decide to hire a coach.

"There truly is no finish line."
– Joan Benoit Samuelson

This type of learning is designed to get your closer to your goals – business and/or personal. Through consistent output, it will deliver knowledge and skills that ensure you're a little better at something tomorrow than you are today.

Unexpected Learning

Most people are creatures of habit, preferring to be routine oriented. Which is why when the unexpected happens, they either choose to ignore or panic about what the potential consequences could be.

But unexpected learning can be extremely beneficial if you act upon it. It can sometimes contradict a piece of knowledge or understanding you already have. It may make you question the status quo or the way you've been doing something.

As Peter Drucker discusses in his book *Innovation And Entrepreneurship*, the most valuable sources of innovation are often the unexpected experiences.

Whether it's a success or failure, the element of surprise can deliver ideas and insights that allow you to see things with more clarity or take advantage of a new trend.

It's the same with your comfort zone. No growth is ever achieved within it – you must venture outside.

There's an African proverb that perfectly describes the whole essence of learning, leaning in, playing full out and getting outside your comfort zone:

"Smooth seas do not make skillful sailors."

Don't be afraid of change or the unexpected. Go where the fear is. Always have an open mind, and be willing to change and adapt accordingly.

Now go out and start punching above your weight!

"Success is where preparation and opportunity meet."
– Bobby Unser

Acknowledgements

Many of the thoughts, ideas, strategies and stories in this book are the result of some incredible conversations, experiences and learning I've been grateful to be part of. They have helped me to grow, both personally and professionally.

I would therefore like to thank:

Daniel Priestley, for giving me an entirely different perspective on standing out, scaling up and making a more positive impact in the world.

Errol Abramson, for sharing more than five decades of insights into creating and implementing systems and scalability for any type of business.

Andrew Priestley, for his patience, clarity, results-driven strategic direction and tenacity in holding me accountable.

Andy Kear, for seeing my early potential as a cricketer and putting me in an environment that allowed me to flourish.

Stewart Martyn, for enabling me to enjoy playing football again, and taking my abilities to a whole new level – physically, mentally and tactically.

Gary Vaynerchuk, for serving as a constant reminder that I can and will succeed, and being an inspiration behind the name Hustle22.

I would also like to thank the sports men and women below for reaching the top of their profession, serving as an inspiration to many, and providing the quotes used throughout this book.

Muhammad Ali – former Olympic gold medallist, world heavyweight boxing champion and one of the most celebrated sports figures of the 20th century.

Mario Andretti – winner of the Indy 500, Daytona 500, and Formula One World Championship.

Arthur Ashe – first (and still only) African-American male tennis player to win the US Open and Wimbledon.

Sir Roger Bannister – former middle distance runner and the first person to run a sub-four minute mile.

Matt Biondi – eleven-time Olympic swimming medalist, and former five-time world record holder.

Larry Bird – three-time NBA champion, two-time NBA Finals MVP, 12-time All-Star with the Boston Celtics, and an Olympic gold medallist.

Terry Bradshaw – four-time Super Bowl winner and two-time Super Bowl MVP with the Pittsburgh Steelers.

Lou Brock – two-time World Series champion with the St Louis Cardinals and Baseball Hall of Fame inductee.

Herb Brooks – former American ice hockey player and coach who guided the USA Olympic hockey team to the 'Miracle on Ice' triumph in 1980 at Lake Placid.

Paul Brown – co-founder and the first coach of the Cleveland Browns, who later played a role in founding the Cincinnati Bengals.

Kobe Bryant – 18-time NBA All-Star, 15-time All-NBA Team, five-time NBA champion and twice NBA Finals MVP – all with the Los Angeles Lakers.

Wilt Chamberlain – twice NBA champion, NBA Finals MVP and set the NBA single game scoring record with 100 points (out of his team's score of 169).

Johan Cruyff – capped 48 times by the Netherlands (scoring 33 goals), five-time Dutch footballer of the year and a Ballon d'Or winner on three occasions.

Jack Dempsey – former American professional boxer, world heavyweight champion from 1919 to 1926, and known for his exceptional punching power.

Gail Devers – retired American track and field athlete, three-time Olympic champion and National Track and Field Hall of Fame inductee.

Fred Devito – co-founder of Exhale Spa, teacher of movement for almost 40 years, author and public speaker.

Mike Ditka – former American football player and coach, two-time Super Bowl champion (as a coach and player) and a member of the Pro Football Hall of Fame.

Tony Dorsett – former Dallas Cowboys running back, Super Bowl champion and the first to achieve a 99-yard rushing touchdown in NFL history.

Julius Erving – nicknamed Dr J, former ABA and NBA star, two-time ABA champion, NBA champion, NBA MVP and Basketball Hall of Fame inductee.

Machgielis "Max" Euwe – Dutch chess Grandmaster, World Chess Champion from 1935 to 1937, mathematician and author of over 70 chess books.

Sir Mo Farah – UK's most successful distance runner, four-time Olympic gold medallist and six-time World Championship gold medallist.

Brett Favre – 20-year NFL veteran who was the first quarterback to pass for 500 touchdowns, 70,000 yards and complete 6,000 passes. Winner of Super Bowl XXXI.

Roger Federer – one of the greatest tennis players of all time, holder of several ATP records, with 20 Grand Slam and 97 career ATP titles to his name.

Bob Feller – former MLB pitcher, playing 18 seasons for the Cleveland Indians, World Series champion in 1948 and seven-time MLB strikeout leader.

Andrew Flintoff – nicknamed Freddie, former Lancashire and England cricketer who took 226 test wickets and was part of the famous Ashes winning team of 2005.

Adam Gilchrist – arguably the greatest wicketkeeper–batsman in cricket history, played 96 tests for Australia, scoring 5,570 at an average of 47.60 with 379 catches.

Wayne Gretzky – Canadian former professional ice hockey player and head coach, four-time Stanley Cup winner and holder or co-holder of 61 NHL records.

George Halas – founder and former owner of the National Football League's Chicago Bears. As their coach, led them to six NFL championships in four different decades.

Laird Hamilton – American big-wave surfer, co-inventor of tow-in surfing, who left modeling to pursue a career on surfing's World Championship Tour at the age of 17.

Bryce Harper – professional baseball player with the Washington Nationals, National League Rookie of the Year Award winner in 2012 and five-time All Star.

Damon Hill – British former racing driver, who joined the Williams Formula One team in 1992 and amassed 22 career race wins and one world championship.

Ben Hogan – one of the greatest golfers in history with 64 PGA tournament wins, including The Open, The Masters Tournament (twice) and the US Open (four times).

Lou Holtz – during a career that spanned over 40 years, he coached nine college football teams and one NFL team, winning four college championships.

Evander Holyfield – former world cruiserweight, heavyweight champion and
became the first boxer in history to win a version of the heavyweight title four times.

Sir Chris Hoy – former track cyclist, eleven-time world champion, six-time Olympic champion and the second most decorated Olympic cyclist of all time.

Clara Hughes – Canadian cyclist and speed skater, one of only five people to have podium finishes in the Winter and Summer Olympic games.

LeBron James – one of the greatest basketball players of all time, hat-trick of NBA titles and NBA Final MVP awards, four-time NBA MVP and 14-time NBA All Star.

Billie Jean King – former women's world number one tennis player, with 39 Grand Slam titles to her name: 12 in singles, 16 in women's doubles, 11 in mixed doubles.

Lynn Jennings – retired American long-distance runner, set 5,000 metres world indoor record in 1990, four-time World Cross Country gold medallist.

Dwayne Johnson – AKA The Rock, college football national championship winner, a brief career in the CFL before embarking on a career in wrestling with the WWE.

Michael Jordan – helped guide Chicago Bulls to six NBA titles in 1990s. Six-time NBA Finals MVP, five-times NBA MVP, 14-time NBA All Star, three-time NBA All Star MVP.

Jackie Joyner-Kersee – American retired track and field athlete, six Olympic medals including three gold (heptathlon and long jump) at four different Olympic Games.

Dean Karnazes – American ultra-marathon runner, author, completed 50 marathons in 50 US states in 50 consecutive days in 2006.

Tom Landry – was head coach of the NFL's Dallas Cowboys for 29 consecutive years with 20 consecutive winning seasons - both NFL records, two Super Bowl titles.

Tommy Lasorda – worked with Brooklyn/LA Dodgers for 68 seasons – longer than any other person in MLB history, two-time World Series champion in the 1980s.

Bruce Lee – arguably the most influential martial artists of all time, founder of the martial art Jeet Kune Do, and also appeared in five feature-length films.

Carl Lewis – American former track and field athlete who won nine Olympic gold, one silver, and 10 World Championships medals – including eight gold.

Vince Lombardi – legendary former head coach of the NFL's Green Bay Packers, whom he led to five NFL Championships, as well as the first two Super Bowls.

Ronnie Lott – played 14 seasons in the NFL as a cornerback, free safety and strong safety (most notably with the 49ers), four-time Super Bowl champion.

Peyton Manning – 18-year NFL veteran who played for the Indianapolis Colts and Denver Broncos, leading both to Super Bowl championships.

Conor McGregor – Irish professional mixed martial artist, and the first fighter in UFC history to hold titles in two weight divisions simultaneously.

Rick Mears – retired American race car driver, one of only three men to win the Indianapolis 500 four times, holds 26 career wins and 68 podium places.

Lionel Messi – footballer with Barcelona and Argentina national team, holds records for most goals scored in La Liga (378), La Liga season (50), calendar year (91).

Joe Montana – former NFL quarterback, most notably with the 49ers. Four-time Super Bowl champion, three-time Super Bowl MVP and eight trips to the Pro Bowl.

Rafael Nadal – regarded as the greatest clay-court player in history, winner of 10 French Open titles, three US Opens, two Wimbledon titles, and one Australian Open.

Joe Namath – retired NFL quarterback who famously and boldly guaranteed victory for his New York Jets in Super Bowl III – they beat the Baltimore Colts 16–7.

Gary Neville – retired footballer who spent his entire playing career with Manchester United, winning 20 trophies and 85 caps for England.

Bill Nicholson – former English footballer and manager of Tottenham Hotspur, won eight trophies in 16 seasons including the Double-winning season of 1960–61.

Ken Norton – American professional boxer who competed from 1967 to 1981, winning 50 out of 58 career bouts including the WBC heavyweight title in 1978.

Brian O'Driscoll – Irish former rugby union star, captained Ireland from 2003 to 2012 and the British and Irish Lions in 2005. Scored 46 tries for his country.

Shaquille O'Neal – played for six NBA teams in a 19-year career, Rookie of the Year in 1992–93, four-time NBA champion, three-time NBA Finals MVP.

Michael Owen – former footballer, most notably with Liverpool, Real Madrid and Manchester United, 158 career Premier League goals, 89 England caps and 40 goals.

Manny Pacquiao – Filipino professional boxer, the first in history to win major world titles in four weight classes: flyweight, featherweight, lightweight and welterweight.

Danica Patrick – American professional racing driver, the most successful woman ever in American open-wheel racing, only female to win an IndyCar Series race.

Pelé – legendary Brazilian footballer, winner of three FIFA World Cups, Brazil's all-time leading goal scorer (77 goals), voted World Player of the Century.

Gary Player – South African professional golfer, US Masters winner three times, three-time winner of The Open, two-time PGA Champion and won US Open in 1965.

Steve Prefontaine – former American middle and long-distance runner, held USA records in seven different distance track events, from 2,000 to 10,000 metres.

Paula Radcliffe – English long-distance runner, competed in four Olympics, winner of three London Marathons, three New York Marathons and one Chicago Marathon.

Sir Steve Redgrave – most successful male rower in Olympic history, winning the gold at five consecutive games, plus three Commonwealth Games gold medals.

Dan Reeves – former NFL player and coach, who in 38 years in the league participated in nine Super Bowls (the second-most in NFL history), winning two.

Jerry Rice – retired NFL wide receiver, considered the greatest to play the game, holds over 100 NFL records, three-time Super Bowl champion, Super Bowl MVP.

Pat Riley – one of the greatest NBA coaches ever, served as the head coach of five championship teams – four with the LA Lakers and one with the Miami Heat.

Sir Bobby Robson – English football manager, won Dutch and Portuguese leagues, trophies in England and Spain, and took England to the 1990 FIFA World Cup semis.

Ronda Rousey – American wrestler, former MMA star and UFC Women's Bantamweight Champion, first American woman to win an Olympic medal in judo.

Wilma Rudolph – former American sprinter, world-record-holding Olympic champion who won three gold medals at the 1960 Olympic Games.

Babe Ruth – American professional baseball player, holds record for home runs (714), elected into the Baseball Hall of Fame in 1936, one of five inaugural members.

Greg Rutherford – British track and field athlete, winner of long jump gold at 2012 Olympics, 2014 Commonwealth Games and 2015 World Athletics Championships.

Joan Benoit Samuelson – American marathon runner, won gold at the 1984 Olympics, holds the fastest time for an American woman in the Olympic Marathon.

Deion Sanders – AKA Primetime, former NFL (five different teams) and MLB (four teams) star, twice Super Bowl champion and eight-time NFL Pro Bowler.

Michael Schumacher – retired German Formula One driver, winner of seven World Championships (including five in a row), 91 career wins and 155 podium places.

Arnold Schwarzenegger – winner of five Mr Universe titles (first one aged just 20), seven Mr Olympia titles, Governor of California from 2003 to 2011.

Bill Shankly – manager of Liverpool FC, took them from the Second Division to win three First Division titles, two FA Cups, four Charity Shields and one UEFA Cup.

Don Shula – former NFL head coach with an incredible 347 career victories, led the Miami Dolphins to two Super Bowl wins and the only perfect season in NFL history.

Dean Smith – retired American men's college basketball head coach of 36 years with University of North Carolina, achieved 879 victories and two NCAA Division titles.

Mark Spitz – an American former swimmer, nine-time Olympic champion – including seven in Munich in 1972, former world record-holder in seven events.

Sachin Tendulkar – former Indian cricketer and captain, only player to score 100 international centuries, holds record for most number of runs in Tests and ODIs.

Bobby Unser – an American former automobile racer, five times winner of the Indy 500 (across three decades) and twice USAC National Champion.

Lindsey Vonn – alpine skier on the US Ski Team, winner of four World Cup championships, Olympic gold in 2010 and eight World Cup downhill titles.

Shane Warne – retired Australian international cricketer, took over 1,000 international wickets (Tests and ODIs), also scored over 3,000 Test runs.

Venus Williams – American professional tennis player, winner of seven Grand Slam singles titles, has reached 16 Grand Slam finals and has 49 career titles.

John Wooden – former American basketball player and head coach of the UCLA Bruins, led them to ten NCAA national championships in a 12-year period.

Kristi Yamaguchi – American former figure skater who in ladies singles achieved Olympic gold in 1992, also a two-time World champion (1991 and 1992).

Don Zimmer – former MLB player (five teams) and coach (eight teams), winning six World Series, two-time All Star and member of the Boston Red Sox Hall of Fame.